IMPORTANT

The Lüscher Colour Test, despite the ease and speed with which it can be administered, is a 'deep' psychological test, developed for the use of psychiatrists, psychologists, physicians and those who are professionally involved with the conscious and unconscious characteristics and motivations of others. It is most emphatically NOT a weapon to be used in a general contest of 'one-upmanship'.

NOTE

BEFORE PROCEEDING
TO THE TEXT
READ THE INSTRUCTIONS
AT THE BEGINNING
OF THE BOOK

Preliminary instructions for conducting the colour test

1. Remove the eight colour cards from between pages 104–5 and separate them by cutting along the white lines. Shuffle them and lay them out – colour side up – in front of you.

2. Look the eight colours over and decide which colour you like best. *DO NOT try to associate the colour with something else*, such as dress materials, furnishings, automobiles, etc. Just choose the colour for which you feel the most sympathy out of the eight colours in front of you.

3. Pick the chosen card and place it – colour side down – above and to the left of the remaining seven.

4. Look at the remaining colours, choose the one which you *now* like best out of those that are visible and place it – colour side down – beside and to the right of your previous choice.

5. Repeat number 4 with the remaining colours one by one, until all eight are in a row, colour side down, with the most-liked colour on the left and the least-liked colour on the right.

6. Read off, from left to right, the numbers appearing on the backs of the cards and write them down in order on a piece of paper.

7. Pick up the eight colour cards, re-shuffle them, and lay them out again – colour side up – in front of you.

8. Repeat numbers 2 to 6. *DO NOT* consciously try to remember or reproduce your first selection. (Neither should you make a conscious effort *not* to reproduce it.) Just choose the colours as if you were seeing them for the first time.

9. Write down the numbers of the second selection on the same piece of paper as the first, below the numbers already recorded. (Do not lose this piece of paper, as you will need these recorded selections after you have read the text.)

Preliminary interpretation

1. Having made your two selections, you will have two series of eight numbers one below the other, for example:

5 1 4 3 2 0 6 7
1 4 5 2 3 6 0 7

2. Divide each row up into pairs, the first pair being marked '+', the second pair '×', the third pair '=', and the fourth pair '—'. In the example, this will result in the following groups:

+5+1 ×4×3 =2=0 −6−7
+1+4 ×5×2 =3=6 −0−7

3. Additionally, the first and last figure in each row constitute a fifth group, which is marked '+ —'. This gives two more groups.:

+5−7 and +1−7.

4. Turn to Table 1 of the Interpretation Tables (p 104) which gives the interpretation of '+' functions, and read the interpretations for groups +5+1 and +1+4.
5. Table II (p 116) will provide the interpretations for the '×' functions.
Table III (p 127) gives the interpretations for the '=' functions.
Table IV (p 138) gives the interpretations for the '—' functions.
Table V (p 174) gives the interpretations for the '+ —' functions.

(*NOTE: the second selection usually occurs more spontaneously and is therefore more valid than the first selection, especially in doubtful cases.*)

6. Now that your colour selections are on record, go ahead and read the text. Then, if you choose, you can re-group and mark your selections as described in Chapters 3 and 4, and make a more comprehensive analysis.

The
LÜSCHER
colour test

translated and edited by Ian A. Scott

based on the original German text by Dr Max Lüscher

Pan Books
London and Sydney

Dr Max Lüscher and the publishers wish to thank
Mr E. A. Cohn and Miss Susan Gyarmati for their generous assistance
in translating the original test

First published in Great Britain 1970 by Jonathan Cape Ltd
This edition published 1971 by Pan Books Ltd,
Cavaye Place, London SW10 9PG
4th printing 1977
© Max Lüscher 1969
Lüscher Test copyright Test-Verlag, Basel, Switzerland, 1948, 1969
ISBN 0 330 02908 X
Made and printed in Great Britain by
Cox & Wyman Ltd, London, Reading and Fakenham

CONTENTS

Summary of rules for marking anxieties
and compensations
The 'actual problem'
Ambivalence
The rejected or suppressed characteristic
'Emotional' personalities
Conflict between objective and behaviour
Instability of the autonomic nervous system
Work and exhaustibility

The Lüscher Colour Test

INSTRUCTIONS FOR CONDUCTING THE TEST

NOTE: The 'simple' method of performing the Lüscher Colour Test, described in the first three pages of this book, is usually quite sufficient in providing a reasonably accurate interpretation. The method outlined below, and amplified in Chapters Three and Four, is considerably more complex, but it does yield more comprehensive and dependable information about the person being tested, and is therefore to be preferred for professional use.

A. Self-administration of the test:
1. Remove the eight colour cards from between pages 104–5.
2. Shuffle the cards and lay them out – colour side up – in a semi-circle in front of you.
3. Look the eight colours over and decide which colour you like best. *Do not try to associate the colour with something else*, such as dress materials, furnishings, automobiles. Just choose the colour for which you feel the most sympathy out of the eight colours in front of you.
4. Pick up the chosen card and place it – colour side down – above and to the left of the remaining seven.
5. Look at the remaining colours, choose the one which you now like the best out of those which are visible and

place it – colour side down – beside and to the right of your previous choice.

6. Repeat 5 with the remaining colours, until all eight are in a row, all colour side down, with the most-liked colour on the left and the least-liked colour on the right.

7. Read off, from left to right, the numbers appearing on the backs of the cards and write them down in order on a piece of paper.

8. Pick up the eight cards, reshuffle them, and once again lay them out – colour side up – in front of you.

9. Repeat 3 to 6 with this second series of eight colours. *DO NOT* try to remember or to reproduce your first selection. (Neither should you make a conscious effort *not* to reproduce it.) Choose the colours as though you were seeing them for the first time.

10. When the second row is completed, read off the numbers from left to right and write them down on the same piece of paper as the first, beneath the numbers already recorded.

11. Group and mark the two selections as described in Chapter Four.

12. Fill in the rows marked 'C' or 'A' and 'I' following the rules set out in Chapter Five.

13. Analyse the Test (see examples in Chapter Eight).

B. If you are administering the test to someone else, proceed as follows:

1. The eight colour cards are arranged in front of the person taking the test.

2. Say something to this effect: 'Without trying to relate these colours to anything else, but just as colours, which of these do you like best?' Have the person indicate the preferred colour and remember to thank or acknowledge him for his choice.

3. Remove this card and place it – colour side down – at the beginning of a row in front of *yourself*.

4. Then say: 'Of the colours which remain, which do you now like best?' When this has been indicated, acknowledge that, remove the card and place it – colour side down – beside and to the right of the first one.

5. Continue in the same way with the remaining cards until only two are left; then say: 'Of these two remaining cards, which do you prefer?' When indicated, acknowledge, take both cards and place them correctly in the 7th and 8th positions.

6. Record on a piece of paper the numbers of these eight cards in the order in which they appear from left to right.

7. Pick up the eight cards, reshuffle them, and once again arrange them in front of the person being tested.

8. Begin the second series by saying: 'I want you to look at these colours as though you had never seen them before. Don't make a conscious effort to remember or duplicate what you did last time. Which colour do you now like best?'

9. Repeat 3 to 5 above.

10. Record the numbers of the second selection below the numbers already recorded.

11. Group, mark and analyse the selections (as in items 11 to 13 of Method A for the self-administered test).

CHAPTER ONE

COLOUR PSYCHOLOGY

While colour has always surrounded mankind on every side and subjected him to its influence since time immemorial, it is only comparatively recently that we have been able to produce and use colour as freely as we do today. Before the nineteenth century only a limited number of dyes and pigments were known and these were mainly of organic origin. They were also very expensive, so that colourful fabrics and decorative materials were the prerogative of the wealthy. Hundreds of thousands of snails gave their lives so that a Roman emperor could wear his robe of Tyrian purple while his subjects had to be content with unbleached cotton or linen, hides or wool.

Only within the last hundred years or so has this picture changed materially, first with the synthesis of the aniline dyes, later with coal-tar derivatives and metallic oxides, so that today few of the things we make are left in their original manufactured state without being stained, painted or coloured, either wholly or in part. Now there are literally thousands of colours of every imaginable hue and intensity readily available for almost any purpose. Not only do we now have the blue of the sky, the red of the sunset, the green of the trees and all the other colours of nature, but in addition man-made articles, neon lights, paints, wallpapers and colour TV either enchant or assail us continuously.

This increasing use of colour combined with the ever-growing competition between manufacturers looking to increase their sales has led to much development in the field of colour psychology, although, when it comes to marketing, much of this research has been along lines of trial and error. The sugar manufacturer knows, for example, that he must not try to sell his product in a green package, while beauty preparations in a brown jar will remain on the shelf long after others have gone. The colours of nature have had their influence on us, and these influences are deep-seated in our physiological and psychological make-up – but there they are, whether we like them or not. In the case of the things we buy, however, we are free to choose, to exercise our own likes and dislikes, our tastes and our conventions.

It is these that the manufacturer must study to ensure that we reach for his product in preference to that of his competitors. If his product is sugar, then he knows that he must package it in a blue container or at least have blue prominently on the package somewhere, that he must avoid green at all costs, but very probably he does not know why this is so. Yet the physiological sensation associated with the colour blue is 'sweetness'; green, on the other hand, is 'astringence', and who would want astringent sugar? The airline whose passengers refuse to fly with any other line may have the best safety record, or the best aircraft, or the politest hostesses, but the chances are that they have employed the services of a good colour-consultant. Where the colours used for the interior decoration of the cabin have been correctly chosen, then the tensions which are associated with flying in even the most nonchalant of passengers are relaxed to some degree, imposing less nervous strain on them and delivering them at their destination in a comparatively relaxed state.

In regarding a painting or a coloured photograph the psychological significance of colour is usually less apparent because so many other factors are involved – subject matter, balance of shape or form, balance of the colours themselves, the education and expertise of the beholder, and aesthetic appreciation. It is sometimes possible to deduce personality characteristics of a painter when great emphasis is placed on one or two colours – for example, Gauguin's obsession with yellow in his later paintings – but in general, when many colours are used to create some whole, then it is aesthetic judgement which evaluates that whole and determines whether we like it or not, rather than our psychological reaction to particular colours.

In the case of single colours it is possible to be far more specific, especially when the colours have been accurately chosen for their direct association with psychological and physiological needs, as they have in the Lüscher Colour Test. In this case, a preference for one colour and a dislike for another means something definite and reflects an existing state of mind, of glandular balance, or of both. To see how this can be so, why this relationship is universal and why it exists independent of race, sex or social environment, it is necessary to look back at man's long exposure to the colours of Nature.

The Origin of Colour Significance

In the beginning man's life was dictated by two factors beyond his control: night and day, darkness and light. Night brought about an environment in which action had to cease, so man repaired to his cave, wrapped himself in his furs and went to sleep, or else he climbed a tree and made himself as comfortable as he could while awaiting the coming of dawn. Day brought an environment in which action was possible, so he set forth once more to replenish his store and forage or hunt for his food. Night brought passivity, quiescence and a general slowing down of metabolic and glandular activity; day brought with it the possibility of action, an increase in the metabolic rate and greater glandular secretion, thus providing him with both energy and incentive.

The colours associated with these two environments are the dark-blue of the night sky and the bright yellow of daylight.

Dark-blue is therefore the colour of quiet and passivity, bright yellow the colour of hope and activity, but because these colours represent the night and day environments, they are factors which control man rather than elements he can control; they are therefore described as 'heteronomous' colours – that is, colours which regulate from outside. Night (dark-blue) compelled activity to cease and enforced quiescence; day (bright yellow) allowed activity to take place but did not compel it.

To primitive man, activity as a rule took one of two forms – either he was hunting and attacking, or he was being hunted and defending himself against attack: activity directed towards conquest and acquisition or activity directed towards self-preservation. The outgoing actions of attack and conquest are universally represented by the colour red; self-preservation by its complement, green.

Since his actions, whether of attack (red) or defence (green) were at least under his control, these factors and colours are described as 'autonomous', or self-regulating. On the other hand, attack being an acquisitive and out-going action is considered to be 'active', while defence, being concerned only with self-preservation, is considered to be 'passive' (no matter how much action may be involved in trying to subdue a sabre-toothed tiger with a club!).

The Physiology of Colour

Experiments in which individuals are required to contemplate psychologically pure-red for varying lengths of time have shown that this colour has a decidedly stimulating effect on the nervous system – blood pressure increases, respiration rate and heartbeat both speed up. Red is, therefore, 'exciting' in its effect on the nervous system, especially on the sympathetic branch of the autonomic nervous system. Similar exposure to psychologically pure-blue on the other hand has the reverse effect – blood pressure falls, heartbeat and breathing slow down. Dark-blue is therefore 'calming' in its effect and operates chiefly through the parasympathetic branch of the autonomic nervous system.

[The complicated networks of nerves and fibres by which the body and all its parts are controlled can be included under two main headings – the Central Nervous System (CNS) and the Autonomic (or 'self-regulating') Nervous System (ANS).

The central nervous system can be considered – with reasonable accuracy – as concerning itself with those physical and sensory functions which occur at, or above, the threshold of awareness. The autonomic nervous system, on the other hand, is concerned primarily with those functions which take place *below* the threshold of awareness and – for this very reason – must operate on an automatic, self-regulating basis. The beating of the heart, the rise and fall of the lungs, the digestion of food, in fact all the complex processes of the body which must continue without any conscious effort are functions of the autonomic nervous system.

The ANS is composed of two complementary branches acting, in the main, in opposition to one another: the sympathetic nervous system and the parasympathetic nervous system, the fibres from both systems running to each of the organs in which self-regulation is essential. The heartbeat, for example, normally occurs at a rate kept within certain bounds by the balance struck between these two branches of the autonomic nervous system; but under the influence of physical (eg, exertion, effort) or emotional (eg, fear, anger, excitement) effects, the sympathetic system will override the parasympathetic and the heartbeat will speed up. In general terms, the sympathetic

17

nervous system overrides the parasympathetic nervous system under the influence of excitement, exertion or increased necessity. The parasympathetic nervous system works to restore things to normal when conditions of stress have been removed and is the dominant branch of the autonomic nervous system in conditions of calm, contentment and relaxation.]

Even today, the mechanism by which colour is actually 'seen' and recognized as colour is imperfectly understood. When a simple question, such as, 'How do we see colour?' gives rise to so many different theories in the search for an answer, then the chances are that in some way we cannot quite comprehend we are either asking the wrong question or are starting off with some faulty premises. However, the 'contrast theory' of the physiologist Hering seems to fit most closely with what is actually observed in the use of the Colour Test.

Hering observed that 'visual purple' (a substance contained in the rods of the retina within the eye, and also known as 'rhodopsin') was bleached under the influence of bright colours and reconstituted itself when exposed to dark colours – that 'light' had a catabolic (breaking-down) effect, while 'dark' had an anabolic (building-up, regenerative) effect. According to Hering, white subjected visual purple to catabolism and broke it down; black, on the other hand, brought about anabolism and restored visual purple to its original state. The same effects were found to occur with red-green and with yellow-blue, resulting in a 'contrast effect' applicable to all colours in terms of their brightness or darkness.

The Development of Colour Vision

A newly born child developing the ability to 'see' begins by being able to distinguish contrast, that is: 'brightness' and 'darkness'; next comes the ability to distinguish movement, and after that shape and form. The recognition of colour is the last development of all. The distinction of contrast is therefore the earliest and most primitive form of visual perception.

In Man, the more sophisticated interpretations of what his senses tell him appear to be functions of the more 'educated' part of the brain – the cortex. To be able to recognize and distinguish one perfume from another would be a 'cortical' function and the result of educating the sense of smell; but the instinctive reaction to a 'bad smell' is just that – instinctive and reactive, leading at the least to a nose-wrinkling recoil, and at the worst to nausea and vomiting. These are not cortical reactions, but arise in centres in the older and more primitive areas of the brain lying more centrally and which are more closely allied to the brains of our evolutionary ancestors.

Colour vision is similarly related to both educated and primitive brain, as was shown by Becker in 1953, when he proved that a network of nerve fibres led directly from a nucleus in the retina to the midbrain (mesencephalon) and to the pituitary system.

[The pituitary is an endocrine, or ductless, gland lying close to the centre of the brain which secretes several important hormones into the bloodstream. The importance of this gland is such that it is referred to as 'the leader of the endocrine orchestra' and controls the functions of other ductless glands, as well as serving other purposes such as growth control.]

The distinguishing of colour, its identification, naming and any aesthetic reactions to it, are all functions of the cortex; they are therefore the result of development and education rather than of instinct and reactive response. Reflexive and instinctive visual functions on the other hand appear to follow Becker's neural network to the much more primitive midbrain, operating in terms of contrast and affecting the physical and glandular systems through the pituitary in some way which has yet to be fully understood.

'Colour Blindness' Makes No Difference

It is this last factor – the instinctive response to colour in terms of contrast – which makes the Lüscher Test a valid instrument even in cases of defective colour-vision or even actual colour blindness, since the acceptability of a particular colour is somatically (from Greek 'soma', body; somatic therefore means 'having to do with the body') related to the degree to which anabolism or catabolism is needed by the organism. If it is psychically or physically in need of emotional peace, physical regeneration and release from tension or stress, then the instinctive response will be to choose the darker colours. If the organism needs to dissipate energy by outgoing activity or in mental creativeness, then the instinctive response will be for the brighter colours.

An examination into the validity of the Lüscher Test in the event of colour blindness was carried out by L. Steinke, using normal controls and individuals suffering from both partial and total red-green colour blindness.* His findings show that 'colour vision need not be considered in the Lüscher Test at all'.

The Lüscher Test

In stating preferences for this colour or for that, choice is often dictated by circumstances. If the circumstances are the choice of a dress to wear, a wallpaper for the living-room,

* L. Steinke: *Farbpsychologische Untersuchen mit dem Lüscher-test bei angeborenen Farbsinnstörungen, Confinia Psychiatrica,* Vol 3, No 2 (1960).

a paint for the kitchen cupboards, then the resultant choice is determined not only by psychological preference or physiological need (though these will inevitably play a part), but by aesthetic considerations: will the dress go with general colouring or figure? what does the wallpaper do to the curtains and furniture? and so forth.

When, as in the Lüscher Test, colours are presented for choice without involvement of one with the other, then aesthetic judgement becomes subordinate to personal preference, with no need to try to harmonize them with one another, nor to refer the colours to some other frame of reference. It is desirable, just the same, when the test is being given to someone else to suggest that the colours should be selected just as colours, without mental value-judgements as to their suitability for dress materials, furnishings or the upholstery of a new automobile.

In the 'Full' Lüscher Test there are seven different panels of colours, containing in all seventy-three colour-patches, consisting of twenty-five different hues and shades, and requiring forty-three different selections to be made. The resulting test-protocol affords a wealth of information concerning the conscious and unconscious psychological structure of the individual, areas of psychic stress, the state of glandular balance or imbalance, and much physiological information of great value either to the physician or to the psychotherapist. The complete test takes only five to eight minutes, which makes it probably the speediest test on record, while its administration is so simple that it can be taught to almost anyone in half an hour. However, the interpretation of the Full Test requires training and considerable psychological insight. For this reason, this 'Introduction' includes only one of the seven panels – the so-called 'Eight-colour Panel'.

This shortened version of the test is known as the 'Quick Test' or the 'Short Lüscher Test' and though not nearly so comprehensive nor so revelatory as the Full Test, it is still of considerable value in highlighting significant aspects of the personality, and in drawing attention to areas of psychological and physiological stress where they exist. Physicians in Europe use this short version of the test as a useful aid to diagnosis, since it has been found that such stresses show up in the Lüscher Test often long before their physiological results make themselves evident; in this, the test provides them with an incomparable 'early warning system' of stress ailments in their early stages – ailments such as cardiac malfunction, cerebral attack or disorders of the gastrointestinal tract.

The physician is a busy man who has little time to spare for diagnostic media additional to those which are his normal complement, nor for the learning of complicated methods of test interpretation. With the Short Lüscher Test he can with little trouble assign the actual administration of the test to his nurse-receptionist, and with a little practice on his own part tell at a glance whether his patient has a normal test or whether there are signs of stress in areas which should be further investigated.

Quoting from Dr J. Erbslöh in his paper on 'The Use of the Lüscher Colour-Test in Medical Practice':* 'We have to thank Professor Lüscher for his clear recognition of the psychological significance of colours and for the development of a colour test whose special advantage is its simplicity. It is administered by midwives in my delivery ward and by secretaries in my practice. The interpretation of the colours remains the province of the physician.' After giving several examples of the test's advantages for 'early warning' when other methods of diagnosis had proved unproductive, he goes on to say: 'The test deepens the doctor's understanding of the patient's psychological make-up and enables him to be less biased in his judgements. It gives important indications for use in diagnosis and therapy and also for the

* Dr J. Erbslöh: Die Verwendung des Lüscher Farbtests in der ärtzlichen Praxis, Artzliche Praxis, No 31 (1962).

prognosis of certain illnesses. Because of its simplicity and reliability it can be recommended for general use.'

Its use in education is varied and extensive, and numerous investigations into this aspect have been carried out by Karlheinz Flehinghaus and others. Ethnological (H. Klar; H. & N. Dietschy), religio-psychological (Bokslag), geronto-logical (Bokslag) and marriage guidance (Canziani) applications of the test have also been comprehensively investigated. Additionally, Lüscher Personnel Services in London, England, has applied the test to the needs of vocational guidance and personnel selection for industry and commerce (Scott).

The test has been improved and refined since its inception more than twenty years ago, but today it is substantially the same as it was when first introduced. Interpretation has improved and become more comprehensive, but the original premises have withstood the test of time and it has not been necessary to change them in any way.

One of the largest correspondence schools in Europe has found a novel use for the Quick Test – all applicants for courses are tested and the results used to help in advising which courses and occupations the tests suggest would be the best to take up.

Mention has already been made of the four colours: blue, yellow, red and green. These are 'psychological primaries' and constitute what are called the four 'basic colours' of the test. In the Eight-colour Panel of the Quick Test there are, of course, four more. These 'auxiliary colours' are: violet, which is a mixture of red and blue; brown, which is a mixture of yellow-red and black; a neutral grey, containing no colour at all and therefore free from any affective influence, while its intensity places it halfway between light and dark so that it gives rise to no anabolic nor catabolic effect – it is psychologically and physiologically neutral; and finally, black, which is a denial of colour altogether.

CHAPTER TWO

FUNCTIONAL PSYCHOLOGY

The name 'Functional Psychology' has been given to the theories relating colour choice to personality psychology. In the Lüscher Colour Test, the 'structure' of a colour is constant; it is defined as the 'objective meaning' of that colour and remains the same for everyone – dark-blue, for instance, means 'peace and quiet' regardless of whether one likes the colour or dislikes it. The 'function', on the other hand, is the 'subjective attitude towards the colour' and it is this which varies from person to person, and it is the 'function' on which the test interpretations are based. One person may like a particular colour, another may find the same colour boring, a third may be indifferent to it, while a fourth may find it definitely distasteful.

In the test the person being tested (or testing himself) selects the colours in descending order of preference; the colour he likes best and places in the first position is thus the one for which he has the greatest sympathy; that which he chooses last and places in eighth position is the one for which he has greatest antipathy (or least sympathy). By observing where in the row a colour occurs, we can determine what 'function' the particular colour represents, since the subjective attitude towards the various colours varies from greatest to least sympathy.

At the beginning of the row the attitude is one of decided preference, followed by an area which is still one of preference but is less marked; next comes an area regarded as 'indifference' followed by the final area, which is one of antipathy or rejection. Symbols are used to mark these areas, as follows:

Strong preference for a colour	Symbol + (plus sign)
Preference for a colour	Symbol × (multiplication sign)
Indifference towards a colour	Symbol = (equals sign)
Antipathy or rejection of a colour	Symbol − (minus sign)

The Significance of the Eight Positions

Bearing in mind that it is necessary to group the colour selections correctly and then to mark up the appropriate symbols, the following attitudes or 'functions' can be generally established when the eight colours have been placed in their order of preference:

1st *position* The most-liked (sympathetic) colour represents a 'turning towards' and is indicated by the + sign (plus). It shows the *essential method*, the *modus operandi*, of the person choosing it, the means which he turns to or adopts to enable him to achieve his objective. For example, with dark-blue in this position the *modus operandi* would be 'calmness'.

2nd *position* This also is usually indicated by the + sign (plus), in which case it shows what the objective actually is. With dark-blue in this position, for instance, the goal for which he is striving is 'peace and quiet'. Depending on the grouping and marking up of the actual test, however, the 2nd position may be marked with an × (multiplication sign), in which case it has a different meaning (see 3rd & 4th positions below). Where only the colour in the 1st position is marked with a +, then the *modus operandi* and the objective are the same – in other words, the adopted means has become an end in itself. Thus, a person is usually calm because he wishes to achieve some particular objective through being calm, such as ensuring that reason should prevail or maintaining a stable environment; but where dark-blue is the only colour marked with a + sign, then calmness has become an end in itself.

3rd & 4th *positions*   These are usually indicated by the multiplication sign (×) and show the 'actual state of affairs', the situation in which he actually feels himself to be, or the manner in which his existing circumstances require him to act. Dark-blue in these positions would show that he feels he is in a peaceful situation or in one in which it is necessary for him to act calmly.

5th & 6th *positions*   These represent 'indifference' and carry the indicator of the = sign (equals). Colours in this area show that their special qualities are neither being rejected, nor are they especially appropriate to the existing state of affairs, but are being held in reserve, as it were, set aside in safekeeping and not currently in operation. An 'indifferent' colour is thus an unestablished quality, suspended as inappropriate, but is in reserve and can be brought quickly back into operation again at any time when circumstances change. Dark-blue in one of these positions shows that 'peace' has been suspended so that an unpeaceful or irritating situation can be brought under control, or at least made more tolerable.

7th & 8th *positions*   These are indicated by the – sign (minus) and represent a 'turning away from'. Colours which are rejected as unsympathetic represent a particular need which there is some special reason for inhibiting, since not to do so would be disadvantageous. In other words, these colours represent a *need which is suppressed out of necessity*. With dark-blue in one of these positions, for example, the need for peace has to remain unsatisfied because – due to unfavourable circumstances – every relaxation, every surrender, every attempt to bring about closer and more harmonious relationships would have unsatisfactory consequences.

If the interpretations in the Tables are read in conjunction with these descriptions it is possible to arrive at an exhaustive analysis satisfactory both to the average reader and to the specialist.

Interpreting the Functions

It can be seen that the colour itself does not change its basic meaning – the structure remains constant. Its position in the row, however, alters considerably the interpretation which must be placed on it when analysing the personality characteristics revealed by the test. These interpretations are given in the Tables at the end of this book.

Every profession which may make use of this test has its own special jargon; not only the psychologist and the marriage guidance counsellor, but also the psychiatrist, the physician, the educational specialist and the criminologist. Each might wish to have these Tables expressed in his own jargon. Additionally, special wordings might be considered desirable for age and sex, for sociological condition and for diagnosis, whether for medical purposes or for the purposes of occupational guidance. To attempt to do this would seriously overload the Tables, and these have therefore been kept as condensed as possible; where the words 'he, him, himself' occur, they should be interpreted as 'she, her, herself' wherever it is appropriate. This avoids the awkwardness of 'he (or she)' and so forth.

To augment the general nature of the Tables, so that more comprehensive and specialized interpretations can be arrived at where this is desired, relatively complete descriptions of the structural meanings of each of the eight colours are given in Chapter Six (page 56 and following).

CHAPTER THREE

THE BASIC AND AUXILIARY COLOURS

Colour-Coding of the Eight Colours

In the Eight-colour Panel, the colours themselves are allotted numbers for ease of reference, and anyone using the test to any great extent is strongly advised to familiarize himself with these numbers. They are:

1 Dark-blue
2 Blue-green } The four BASIC COLOURS – the
3 Orange-red } 'psychological primaries'
4 Bright yellow

5 Violet
6 Brown } The four AUXILIARY COLOURS
7 Black
0 Neutral grey

Categories of the Four Basic Colours

While the general description of the structure of all eight colours is given in Chapter Six, the four basic colours (blue, green, red and yellow) are of special importance, and have particular significances, as follows:

No 1 Dark-blue : represents
and is

'Depth of Feeling'

Concentric
Passive
Incorporative
Heteronomous
Sensitive
Perceptive
Unifying

Its affective aspects are

Tranquillity
Contentment
Tenderness
Love and affection

No 2 Blue-green : represents
and is

'Elasticity of Will'

Concentric
Passive
Defensive
Autonomous
Retentive

Possessive
Immutable

Its affective aspects are

Persistence
Self-assertion
Obstinacy
Self-esteem

No 3 Orange-red : represents
and is

'Force of Will'

Ex-centric
Active
Offensive-aggressive
Autonomous
Locomotor
Competitive
Operative

Its affective aspects are	Desire
	Excitability
	Domination
	Sexuality

No 4 Bright yellow : represents	'Spontaneity'
and is	Ex-centric
	Active
	Projective
	Heteronomous
	Expansive
	Aspiring
	Investigatory
Its affective aspects are	Variability
	Expectancy
	Originality
	Exhilaration

Concentric means 'subjectively concerned' and though this has some of the connotations of 'introversion' it is not the same thing and should not be confused with it. People who are introverted are concentric, but those who are concentric are not necessarily introverted in the usual meaning of the word. To be subjectively concerned is to be exclusively interested in that which is an *extension* of oneself, as well as being interested in the Self. A person who is continuously communicating to others might ordinarily be considered an extrovert, but if it is found that the topic of conversation is invariably his stamp collection or his family, his wife, his children, his job, his trip to Europe, then he is displaying concentricity since he regards all these things as extensions of himself. Let someone try to bring the conversation around to topics of more general interest and he will either interrupt or cease to listen.

Ex-centric means 'objectively concerned' and is more

nearly akin to extroversion than concentricity is to introversion. The ex-centric individual is interested in the environment, in the things and people around him, either from
the point of view of impinging on and causing effects *on* his
environment, or of drawing his stimuli *from* the environment. If the former, he is being causative and therefore
autonomous towards his environment; if the latter, he is
being the effect of his environment and therefore *heteronomous*. *Autonomy* is thus the equivalent of 'being a cause',
while *heteronomy* is equivalent to 'being an effect'.

Passive and *active* carry much the same meanings as concentric and ex-centric, respectively.

Combined Basic Colours

It will be seen that Nos 1 and 2 (blue and green) are both
concentric (passive); where they occur together in the test,
concentricity is being heavily stressed, but whether this is a
desired behaviour pattern, an actual pattern, a latent pattern
or a rejected pattern will, of course, depend on the position
of this combination in the row.

Similarly, Nos 2 and 3 (green and red) are both autonomous (self-regulating, causative); where they occur together
in the test initiative and self-determination are stressed, but,
again, the manner in which they are emphasized will depend
on where they occur.

Nos 3 and 4 (red and yellow) are both ex-centric (active)
and outwardly directed; where they occur together outgoingness is emphasized.

Nos 1 and 4 (blue and yellow) are both heteronomous
(regulated from outside sources), and therefore where they
occur together 'other-determinism' is being stressed.

Each of the above pairs, when they occur together in the
same functional group (both +, both ×, both = or both −)
implies a certain over-emphasis of some characteristic −

concentricity, autonomy, ex-centricity or heteronomy. A
better balance is achieved by the combination of blue and
red (Nos 1 and 3), in which the concentric heteronomy of
blue balances and harmonizes with the ex-centric autonomy
of red. The combination of green and yellow (Nos 2 and 4)
while offsetting the concentric autonomy of green against
the ex-centric heteronomy of yellow, does not provide a
particularly balanced whole. This is due to the fact that the
expansive hopefulness of yellow does not harmonize well
with the self-centred obstinacy of green; this combination
can sometimes introduce its own conflicts.

Basic Colours Should Be Preferred

The four basic colours, blue, green, red and yellow (1, 2, 3
and 4), representing as they do fundamental psychological
needs – the need for contentment and affection, the need to
assert oneself, the need to act and succeed and the need to
look forward and aspire – are all of special importance. They
should therefore all occur in the first four or five places of
the test when selected by a healthy, normally balanced
individual who is free from conflicts and repressions.

The Auxiliary Colours

The auxiliary colours, violet, brown, black and grey (5, 6, 7
and 0) are in a rather different category. Black and grey are,
strictly speaking, not colours at all – black being the negation
of colour and the grey of the test being strictly neutral and
colourless. These two are therefore 'achromatic' (not coloured). Violet is a mixture of blue and red, while brown is a
mixture of orange-red and black, giving a darkish, relatively
lifeless colour (sometimes also classed as 'achromatic'
although this is not strictly accurate). Preference for any of

32

the three 'achromatic colours', black, grey or brown may be taken as indicating a negative attitude towards life; this will be more fully appreciated from a study of the chapter on 'Anxieties'.

Neither the brown nor the violet are psychological primaries and were selected for the test after a great deal of trial and error as colours representative of other characteristics which the individual would *normally* place in the functionally indifferent area of the test or even reject, but which are frequently found to be exaggerated and to surge towards the beginning of the row at the expense of one or other of the basic colours.

An additional purpose served by the inclusion of four auxiliary colours is to increase the overall utility of the test by adding colours found to have universal applicability, thus expanding the range over which the basic colours themselves are spread. This allows a more clearly defined significance to be placed on the location of a colour in the row.

CHAPTER FOUR

GROUPING AND MARKING THE EIGHT-COLOUR SEQUENCE

Where the eight colours are selected once only in their order of preference from most liked to most disliked, there is little alternative but to group them in pairs – the first two colours being marked +, the next pair ×, the third pair =, and the final pair – . While this often results in a reasonably accurate interpretation, there are numerous advantages in going through the eight colours twice.

Wherever possible, two series of selections should be made with a short interval of a few minutes between them. No attempt should be made on the second selection to try deliberately to remember and to reproduce the first sequence of colours. Choices on the second occasion should be made as though the eight colours were now being seen for the first time. People occasionally believe that going through the colours twice is some sort of a 'memory test' – that they are expected to reproduce exactly what they chose the first time. Not only is this not so, but in general it can be said that a second selection which reproduces exactly the first selection indicates the existence of a certain rigidity of attitude and inflexibility of affective nature.

Assuming that a test selection was as follows: 1st, red; 2nd, blue; 3rd, violet; 4th, yellow; 5th, green; 6th, brown; 7th, grey; 8th, black – then the test protocol would be:

3 1 5 4 2 6 0 7

34

If no second selection is made, then the Eight-colour sequence would be grouped and marked as follows:

$$3 \quad 1 \quad 5 \quad 4 \quad 2 \quad 6 \quad 0 \quad 7$$
$$+ \quad + \quad \times \quad \times \quad = \quad = \quad - \quad -$$

and it would be necessary to consult the Interpretation Tables with these groups.

When a second selection is made after a short interval of two or three minutes, it is likely to be slightly different and some of the colours may be transposed, while some may move farther forward or farther back in the row. Where two or more colours change position but still lie alongside a colour which was a neighbour in the first selection, then a group exists, and this is the group which should be encircled and marked with the appropriate function-symbol. These groups will very often differ to some extent from the simple grouping in pairs of the above example.

Assuming that a second selection is made by the same person who made the above choice, we might get the following:

1st selection: 3 1 5 4 2 6 0 7
2nd selection: 3 5 1 4 2 6 7 0

In this case, it will be seen that blue (1) and violet (5) still lie side by side although their mutual position is reversed. The same applies to grey (0) and black (7). Red (3) stays in 1st position in both cases, while yellow (4), green (2) and brown (6) all keep the same position in the second selection as they have in the first. Grouping is therefore carried out as shown below:

35

The rules for marking such test-protocols are:

(1) The first group (or single numeral) is marked +
(2) The second group (or single numeral) is marked ×
(3) The last group (or single numeral) is marked —
(4) The whole of the remainder is marked   =

Where pairs exist, they must be used for interpretative purposes rather than single numerals,* and for this reason the 'indifferent' area (=) in the last example has been divided into two groups (= 4 = 2 and = 2 = 6).

Adopting the above rules for groupings and marking may result in cases in which the colours of the first and second selections are assigned different symbols. In this case, both selections should be separately marked, as follows:

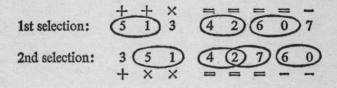

1st selection:

2nd selection:

The second selection usually occurs more spontaneously and is more valid than the first selection, especially in doubtful cases. It is therefore the grouping and marking of the second selection which should be used for entry into the Tables.

A number may be common to two different functional groups, in which case both groups should be interpreted and the protocol marked as shown next:

* If the reader wishes, he may *also* consult the interpretations for the single numeral – provided he considers the colour pair as well.

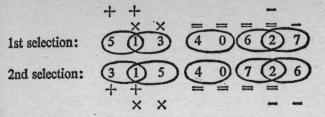

In this last case, the groups to be looked up in the Tables will be: $+ 3 + 1$, $\times 1 \times 5$, $= 4 = 0$, $= 7 = 2$, $- 2 - 6$ (there are also the two additional groups $+ 3 - 6$ and $+ 3 - 2$, but no mention of these has yet been made).

After grouping, it will sometimes be found that two colours of a group in one selection have become separated or split up in the other selection, standing alone and unpaired. When this is so, the single colours are enclosed in a square (see two examples below).

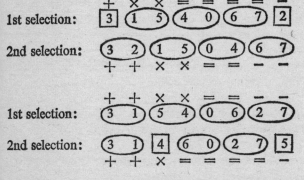

In cases such as this, the Tables should be consulted for the appropriate meanings of both the group and the two colours of the separated pair. In the first example above, the entries for $+ 3 + 2$ and for $+ 3 - 2$ should both be used; in the second example, $\times 4$, $- 5$, and $\times 5 \times 4$ should all be entered and interpreted.

CHAPTER FIVE

ANXIETIES, COMPENSATIONS, AND CONFLICTS

Stress-sources

It has already been mentioned that the four basic colours represent basic psychological needs; they should therefore, in a normal test-protocol, occur at the commencement of the row, or at least within the first five places. When they do not, this is an indication of the presence of some physiological or psychological deficiency which can be considered the more serious the farther back in the row the basic colour is placed.

If a basic colour is rejected by being placed farther back in the Eight-colour sequence than the 5th position, then that particular basic need is remaining unsatisfied because the circumstances are unfavourable. Such an unsatisfied basic need is a 'stress-source' giving rise to a sense of deprivation and thus leading to anxiety. The stress-source of a rejected basic colour therefore shows an anxiety-laden source of psychic or functional disturbance.

Because of this, when one of the basic colours, blue, green, red or yellow, is found in the last three positions of the row (6th, 7th or 8th positions) it is regarded as a rejection and given the indicator — (minus). Any colour occurring later in the row must also be marked —, so that if a basic colour occurs in 6th place, then the colours in 7th and 8th places are both marked – and must also be regarded as rejections producing a degree of anxiety. All rejections representing sources of anxiety are additionally marked by placing the letter 'A' below the minus sign, to draw attention to the fact that anxiety resulting from a stress-source is indicated by the test-protocol.

As an example, let us suppose that red (3) appears in 6th position, followed by brown (6) in 7th position and black (7) in 8th position. Now brown and black in these two positions are quite normal as a general rule, but since the red is a basic colour and appears as far back as the 6th position, then it is a stress-source indicating the presence of anxiety; the brown and black which follow it must therefore also be regarded as anxiety-laden. This is made evident by marking the last three positions as follows:

$$. \quad . \quad . \quad . \quad . \quad \underline{3} \quad \underline{6} \quad \underline{7}$$
$$ A \quad A \quad A$$

Compensations

Often the unsatisfied need and the resulting anxiety become suppressed as emotionally unpleasant so that they are no longer consciously recognized, and often appear as only a vague disquiet. Regardless of the extent to which it may come to conscious awareness, such a stress-source compels a type of compensatory behaviour, which is indicated in the test by the colour chosen in the 1st position. This position, the *essential method*, must always be regarded as compensatory if a basic colour is rejected. To draw attention to this fact, the letter 'C' must be written below the figure in the 1st position whenever an 'A' occurs at the end of the row.

The existence of such a stress-source and the anxiety to

which it gives rise always lead to, and express themselves in, a compensatory mode of behaviour which is compulsive, excessive, permitting of no choice, and occurring as a generalized tendency. Since a compensation of this sort is by its very nature a substitute activity, it seldom leads to any real satisfaction, resulting instead in inappropriate or excessive activity, in pronounced bias and prejudice, in perfectionism and a tendency to moralize to others, in compulsive dilettantism, in speculative argumentation, or in some other form of substitute satisfaction.

When anxieties and stress-sources occur, the 1st position may be occupied by one or another of the four basic colours. In this case, although a compensation is needed for the stress-source, the actual compensation afforded by a basic colour is considered to be more or less 'normal', though it must be remembered that *any* compensatory substitute implies a departure from optimum behaviour since its obsessive character impairs freedom to evaluate existing conditions and act appropriately; rationality has become subordinated to a compulsion to act in a particular way.

Exaggerated Compensations

Of the four auxiliary colours, it has already been said that preference for the so-called 'achromatic' colours brown, grey, or black implies a negative attitude to life. If any of these three colours occur within the *first three* places of the Eight-colour sequence, then not only is compensation present, but the type of compensation can no longer be considered as 'normal', implying instead a special degree of exaggerated behaviour. These colours, and any which precede them in the row, must all be marked + and subscribed with the letter 'C'. If, for example, grey (0) stands in 3rd place and therefore qualifies for a + sign and for a 'C', then the two preceding colours must also be marked + and 'C'. Thus:

$$3 \quad 4 \quad 0 \quad . \quad . \quad . \quad . \quad .$$
$$+ \quad + \quad +$$
$$C \quad C \quad C$$

Sometimes it will occur that grey, brown, or black appears in one of the first three places without a basic colour appearing in positions 6, 7, or 8. When this happens, the last colour in the row (in 8th position) must be regarded as an anxiety, even when that may be the usual place for that particular colour to occur. In other words, when there is an anxiety, there must be a compensation; when there is a compensation, there must be an anxiety.

Intensity of the Anxiety and Compensation

The intensity of existing psychological or physiological deficits giving rise to anxiety is considered to be relatively mild when a basic colour is in the 6th position and relatively serious when in the 8th position. This permits the adoption of a simple rule-of-thumb method of measuring this intensity, by allotting exclamation marks (!) to the stress-source in accordance with the following rules:

(1) Where a basic colour occurs in 6th position – allot 1 !
(2) Where a basic colour occurs in 7th position – allot 2 !!
(3) Where a basic colour occurs in 8th position – allot 3 !!!

A similar method is adopted for measuring the intensity of the compulsion associated with compensations, as follows:

(1) Where a basic colour *or violet* occurs as a compensation – no allotment.

(2) Where grey, brown, or black occurs in 3rd place – allot 1!

(3) Where grey, brown or black occurs in 2nd place – allot 2!!

(4) Where grey, brown or black occurs in 1st place – allot 3!!!

After a test-protocol has been grouped and marked in the usual way, the letters 'C' and 'A' should be subscribed where appropriate, and !s allotted in accordance with these rules:

!!!	!!				!	!!	Total !s = 8
C	C			A	A	A	
+	+	×	×	=	=		
0	6	5	1	3	4	2	7

Example:

7	0	6	1	5	2	4	3
+	+	+	×	×	–	–	–
C	C	C			A	A	A
!!!	!!	!			!	!!	!!!

Total !s = 12

Prognosis

The above example is of an extreme case, showing the maximum possible number of exclamation marks (12) allotted to the second selection. This indicates the existence of many anxieties for which compensation is attempted by intense and irrational behaviour. Since the second selection is more valid for interpretation than the first selection, a comparison of the two provides a ready indication of how a situation may be expected to develop.

Where the second selection shows fewer allotted !s than the first selection, then the general prognosis can be considered favourable. Where the reverse is the case, then the prognosis is less favourable.

A ready 'rule-of-thumb' guide is thus provided for forecasting an individual's response to improved conditions imposing less stress, or to a course of psychotherapy. When the number of !s allotted to the second selection is greater than for the first, then even improved conditions or therapy may resolve problems very slowly or not at all. Where some or all of the anxieties and compensations appearing in the first selection disappear in the second, then the prognosis is better, the trouble is less deep-seated and therefore yields more readily to remedial treatment or to a change in environmental conditions. In the last example, the prognosis is not favourable.

After the Interpretation Tables (on page 189), figures will be found showing the number of !s allotted, from zero to the maximum of twelve, among 1,000 adult 'normal' men and women. These figures are based on British norms.

Summary of Rules for Marking Anxieties and Compensations

(a) The 8th position of the row always represents a repressed need (which may, or may not, constitute an 'anxiety') and therefore always bears the symbol − (minus).

(b) If a basic colour (1, 2, 3 or 4) occurs in 6th, 7th or 8th positions, this, together with any following colours, represents an 'anxiety' providing the motive for a 'compensation'. Each such colour should be marked −, and the letter 'A' subscribed. They reveal the basis or bases of functional or psychic disturbance (stress-sources).

(c) When colours with an 'A' occur, at least the colour in the 1st position should be regarded as a 'compensation' and subscribed with the letter 'C'. The 1st-position colour is always marked with the symbol + (plus).

(*d*) If any of the colours 0, 6 or 7 occurs in positions 1, 2 or 3, this and any preceding colours represent compensations and they should all be marked +, the letter 'C' being written below them.

(*e*) If colours with a 'C' occur, at least the colour in the 8th position must be regarded as an 'anxiety' and subscribed with the letter 'A'.

(*f*) The intensity of the 'anxiety' or of the 'compensation' is marked by the allocation of exclamation marks (!), as follows:

> If a basic colour occurs in 6th position, 1 !; in 7th position, 2 !!; in 8th position, 3 !!!
> If any of the colours 0, 6 or 7 occurs in 3rd position, 1 !; in 2nd position, 2 !!; in 1st position, 3 !!!

The 'Actual Problem'

The existence of an unsatisfied basic need together with the compensation which is the attempt to solve it reveal the type of conflict which is involved. Thus, anxiety plus compensation discloses the 'actual problem'; it is this actual problem or conflict which can provide an entrance point for any psychological or medical therapy, should such be indicated.

There are few of us indeed who go through life with the desirelessness of a Buddhist adept, and therefore most of us want something and wish to avoid something else; this in itself introduces some stress into the task of living, but is quite a normal thing and does not qualify as a 'problem' or as a 'conflict'. It merely provides some tension for us to contend with.

What we want is, by definition, indicated in the Colour Test by the colour(s) in the first or first two positions; what we wish to avoid is, also by definition, shown by the colour in the last position. Combining these two different functions (the + function and the − function) provides us immediately with the method adopted to deal with a stress-source (whether normal, or exaggerated), and a fifth Table, setting out this + − function, has been included in the Interpretation Tables to show what the 'actual problem' is for every possible combination.

'Everybody knows' what a problem is! One's wife or one's husband is a problem, work is a problem, one's mother-in-law is a problem, juvenile delinquency and the rising crime rate are problems. But, in actual fact, *none of these things is a problem at all*! A problem is never a one-sided affair; to be a *problem* it must include a would-be solver – there must be a side which is saying 'how can I solve or deal with' the problem. Thus, one's mother-in-law cannot herself *be* a problem, the problem must include both mother-in-law and the person who is trying to discover *how* to live with her, the operative word for a problem being 'How?'

The 'actual problem' as discovered from the Colour Test obeys this rule. The rejected colour(s) and the anxieties shown by the test indicate the stress-source which the person does not wish to have to tolerate. Whether or not it is suppressed below the level of consciousness, there still remains a disquiet which compels the attempt to deal with it in some compensating manner. The 'How?' of this attempt is indicated by the most favoured colour or group. This combination of stress-source and how to deal with the unease to which it gives rise, together makes up the problem itself. The fact that it is an *attempt to solve*, and not an actual solution, accounts for the continued existence of the problem and, therefore, for the continued effort to solve it by the method adopted.

The interpretations given in Table V show the components of the 'actual problem' – the stress-source itself and the method adopted in the attempt to solve it. In a simple and straightforward test this will involve only the colours in the 1st and 8th positions, but where there are anxieties and

45

compensations then there may be several such 'actual problems' to consider.

In the second example given on page 42, it can be seen that there are three colours marked as compensations and three marked as anxieties, so that we are faced with a great many 'actual problems' (in this case, nine). Some of these will naturally be greater and of more significance than others, but all of them will have some application.

The most significant 'actual problem' will be that comprising the colour in 1st place and the colour in 8th position – in this case, $+ 7 - 3$. The least significant 'actual problem' will be that comprising the compensation farthest from the 1st place and the anxiety farthest from the last place – in this case, $+ 6 - 2$.

It is desirable to have some sort of rule for the assigning of priorities when faced with such a formidable array of 'actual problems', in order that their relative magnitude can be appreciated. Since an 'anxiety' has slightly greater significance than a 'compensation', the order of proceeding is:

Compensation	Anxiety	In quoted example (see page 42)	
1st position	8th position	$+ 7 - 3$	Most significant
1st position	7th position	$+ 7 - 4$	
2nd position	8th position	$+ 0 - 3$	
2nd position	7th position	$+ 0 - 4$	
1st position	6th position	$+ 7 - 2$	
2nd position	6th position	$+ 0 - 2$	
3rd position	8th position	$+ 6 - 3$	
3rd position	7th position	$+ 6 - 4$	
3rd position	6th position	$+ 6 - 2$	Least significant

In the average test-protocol it will rarely be necessary to look up more than four such 'actual problems'. Indeed, it might be said that it is *never* necessary even when there are nine, as in the above example, since the major problems will so swamp the others as to make them of relatively little importance in comparison. However, if a test indicating so seriously negative an attitude should be encountered, then the priorities which should be assigned to the 'actual problems' are as set out above.

Ambivalence

Occasionally a test-protocol will be found in which a colour stands in the 1st or 2nd position in one selection of eight colours and in the 8th or 7th place in the other selection. Such a protocol displays a degree of ambivalence – double value – towards the characteristics of that colour.

For example:

$$
\begin{array}{ccccccc}
 & ! & & & ! & & \text{Total !s} = 2 \\
\text{C} & \text{C} & \text{C} & & \text{A} & \text{A} & \text{A} \\
 & - & - & & - & - & - \\
+ & \times & \times & & = & = & = \\
3 & \boxed{1\ \ 6} & 5 & \boxed{2\ \ 4} & & \boxed{0\ \ 7} & \\
\end{array}
$$

$$
\begin{array}{ccccccc}
\boxed{1\ \ 6} & 5 & \boxed{4\ \ 2} & \boxed{7\ \ 0} & 3 & & \\
+\ \ + & \times & =\ \ = & =\ \ = & - & & \\
\text{C}\ \ \text{C} & & & & \text{A} & & \\
!! & & & & !!!\ \text{Total !s} = 5 & & \\
\end{array}
$$

In the test-protocol above, the colour red (3) appears in 1st place in the first selection and in 8th place in the second selection. This indicates a degree of ambivalence in red – that the characteristics which red signifies are at times favoured and at times rejected.

Combining red in 1st position (+ 3) with red in 8th position (– 3), we get + 3 – 3, and, since they do occasionally occur, these ambivalences are included in the + – Function Table. The group + 3 – 3 is shown there as meaning: 'Denotes an ambivalent attitude varying between the desire to have his own way and the need to be left in peace'.

In the Lüscher Eight-colour Test, these ambivalances are of little significance, because test procedure has been modified to make it more simple as compared with the Full Test, but the sudden retreat or advance of a colour from first to second selection should not be entirely ignored. Bearing in mind that the second selection is always the more valid and important of the two, the above example tells us that though the individual may start off with the desire to 'have his own way', this rapidly disintegrates into a 'peace at any price' attitude. Red vitality becomes depleted quickly under only mild pressure. In this case, even the concentration involved in making the selections is sufficient to bring about this depletion.

The Rejected or Suppressed Characteristic

Of the eight positions in which the colours can be placed, the position conveying most information about the individual is the final or 8th position; that is, the group which is the most informative is the − (minus) group. It is therefore possible to tell a great deal about a person merely from knowledge of the colour, or pair of colours, he likes least. And, for this reason, Table IV (The − Function) is by far the most comprehensive of the various tables and has been compiled in a slightly different fashion from the other four.

Each single colour, and each possible pair of colours, is given two interpretations. The first of these is the 'Physiological interpretation' and indicates the stress-source, which may be normal, mild, serious or very serious. A normal stress-source is one which is neither classed as an 'anxiety', nor accompanied in the Table by one, two or three asterisks. For example, brown and black in 7th and 8th positions represent a normal stress-source; $- 6 - 7$ implies 'a desire to control one's own destiny' and so activity is geared in such a way as to effect this. Such behaviour implies no aberration. A mild stress-source is one in which a 'normal' colour or group has become classed as an 'anxiety', not because of a rejected basic colour, but because grey, brown or black have occurred towards the beginning of the row (see rule *e* on page 44). Serious and very serious stress-sources are those accompanied in the Table by one or more asterisks.

The second interpretation given in the Table is the 'Psychological interpretation' and describes the characteristics and behaviour implied by the rejection of that particular colour or group. The detail given in this section is sometimes so extensive that, in every case, an 'In brief' section has been added in an attempt to summarize the main feature of the group.

'Emotional' Personalities

In an average test-protocol, two, three or even four colours will be found marked with the equals sign ($=$) of 'indifference'. That is to say that the characteristics which these colours represent are not currently in operation, but are held in reserve. As a result, a part – sometimes a large part – of the emotional spectrum is in abeyance, not manifesting itself readily unless there is a decided change in the circumstances. In other words, that part of the emotional spectrum will not be called into play unless something occurs which is important enough to make it necessary. Such a person will be emotionally stable and not likely to display aspects of 'indifferent' emotions without due cause.

Anxiety (A) and Compensation (C), however, 'dramatize' the emotions. Of the eight colours available, a maximum of three can occur as $+$ Compensations and three as $-$

Anxieties, leaving only two colours for the × function of actual situation or behaviour. In such a case, there are no = 'indifferent' colours at all. No part of the emotional spectrum is in abeyance; everything is involved in one way or another. Therefore, emotions are liable to manifest themselves very readily. Moment-to-moment behaviour is far less predictable and tends to be less logical. Thus, where conflict has arisen from anxiety and compensation, 'emotional' behaviour is far more easily aroused by comparatively minor stimuli.

Conflict between Objective and Behaviour

In analysing a test-protocol, consideration should be given to the desired objective (the + positions) and the actual situation or behaviour (the × positions) to see whether any conflict exists between them.

For example, in the protocol

$$
\begin{array}{cccccccc}
1 & 2 & 3 & 4 & 5 & 0 & 6 & 7 \\
+ & + & \times & \times & = & = & - & -
\end{array}
$$

there are all the surface indications of complete normality; the four basic colours occur at the beginning of the test, nothing is subscribed A or C, while the +, ×, =, −, and + − groups, when looked up in the Interpretation Tables, have no asterisks alongside them. What, if anything, is wrong?

Referring back to page 31, the group 1 2 (blue/green), which in this case is the *modus operandi* and the desired objective, is exclusively concentric and subjectively concerned. The essential method is tranquillity (1) and the goal itself is defensive self-possession (2). Yet the existing situation is being handled by ex-centric outgoingness and is so contrary to what is desired that conflict may well arise. In this particular case (it is an actual test), conflict was manifest, the woman in question turning to psychotherapy. She was, in fact, forcing herself to be gay, to follow all the latest fashions, to have her hair done twice a week, to go dancing, to entertain – because she felt this was necessary to keep her husband's interest. She did not want to do any of these things, and, as it later turned out, did not need to. Her husband drew a deep sigh of relief when this conflict was finally resolved!

Instability of the Autonomic Nervous System

A type of disturbance of clinical interest to the physician concerns the stability or instability of the autonomic nervous system. Indications of instability frequently appear in the Colour Test long before its pathological effects are normally evident. The stable self-regulating mechanism of the autonomic nervous system under the control of the sympathetic and parasympathetic branches – which work sometimes together and sometimes in opposition to each other – normally operates within limits which it cannot exceed without danger. Biological regulation either occurs imperceptibly or by rapidly swinging back into line some physiological function which is approaching too close to its safety limit. When this self-regulation occurs as it should the system is considered stable.

The autonomic nervous system is concerned with the regulation of body functions which are not normally under conscious control – digestive processes, the smooth musculature, secretions of various glands and organs, the heart and lungs, peristalsis of the alimentary tract, genitalia, and so forth. Instability in this system can therefore have a multiplicity of effects, often being accompanied by various organic troubles which frequently seem to be quite minor and which may move around the body from one area to another. Such instability can develop into serious malfunctioning unless something is done about it. The Colour Test provides a means of diagnosing the presence of self-regulating instability in its very early stages, allowing prompt remedial action to be taken in time to prevent the development of serious pathological conditions.

From what was said on pages 16–18 concerning the anabolic and catabolic effects of light and dark, we saw that there was a relationship between the somatic needs of the body and the choice of light or dark colours. In the test, the two brightest colours are the yellow (4) and the red (3); the two darkest are the black (7) and the blue (1). Therefore, if the test-protocol shows the group 3 4 (or 4 3) at or near one end of the row, with the group 1 7 (or 7 1) at or near the other, then it can be assumed that self-regulating instability is present. Where the group 3 4 or 4 3 is at the beginning and the group 1 7 or 7 1 towards the rear, this instability, though present, has not necessarily reached the stage of being serious. Where the reverse is the case, with the dark colours at the beginning and the bright at the end, instability has been present for a considerable time and may have led to pathological deterioration.

Work and Exhaustibility

Three of the four basic colours are directly concerned, amongst other things, with ability to maintain optimum effectiveness over periods of time. These three are: green (2), red (3) and yellow (4), and the group 2 3 4 (or any combination of these three colours in juxtaposition) is called the 'work group'. Blue (1), as a passive and tranquil colour, is not associated with work but with peace and contentment.

The parts played by the three colours of the work-group in their capacity of originating and maintaining effective operation are as follows:

Green   provides the 'elasticity of will' which allows one
          to persist despite opposition or difficulties, be-
          cause by persisting one can accomplish the task
          and thus enhance one's own self-esteem.

Red   provides the 'force of will' that desires action and
          effectiveness, the satisfaction that comes from
          having moulded something to suit oneself.

Yellow   provides the 'spontaneous' enjoyment of action,
          the ability to project oneself and the expectancy
          which looks forward to the outcome of the job –
          and even beyond it to the new and interesting
          jobs which may be awaiting the completion of
          the present one.

Ideally, then, this work-group should stand together in
the test and should occur at or towards the beginning of the
row. When they are together and towards the front, then it
is safe to say that work will be done well and will be well
integrated, *providing it is the sort of work that the person
wants to do.* Assuming that it is, long periods of work and
the occurrence of difficulties and problems in carrying it
through will have little effect; they will be tackled and overcome until the task is satisfactorily completed.

The personal priorities with which an individual may
approach a task will be indicated in the test by the colour of
the work-group which he puts first. If it is green, then his
purpose is to increase his self-esteem and his stature in the
eyes of others; if red, it is his desire to feel that he has won a
battle over something which he decided to tackle; if yellow,
then it is because he enjoys projecting himself into something
in which he can be interested.

Unfortunately, the work-group very frequently does not
stand together as an integrated whole. Sometimes two of the
three colours are together while the third is separated; less
frequently, all three of the colours are widely separated. In
this latter case the 'work prognosis' is not very good for the

type of work in which the individual is engaged, but it is necessary to examine both first and second selections to see in what way the work-group has changed in the short period which elapsed between them.

For example:

```
                              !!   Total !s = 2
    C                         A    A
                              —    —
    +   +   ×   ×   =   =   =
    3   4   2   5   0  (6   1)  7
    3   0   4   5  (6   1)  2   7
    +   +   ×   ×
                              —    —   —
    C   C                     A    A   A
        !!                    !    !!   Total !s = 5
```

In this case, several things are noticeable. Firstly, the work-group in the first selection is intact and right at the beginning, while in the second selection it has disintegrated. Secondly, the group 3 4 stands at the beginning of the first selection while the group 1 7 stands at the end, implying instability of the self-regulating nervous system. Thirdly, the second selection has five exclamation marks (!), compared with only two in the first selection, indicating that even minor stresses or concentration give rise to conflict. Fourthly, the desire for action and effectiveness (red) is compensatory in both selections and therefore not necessarily appropriate to a particular task. Finally, the green tenacity and persistence (2) falls right away from 3rd to 7th place where it actually becomes a stress-source leading to anxiety.

Summing up, this test shows an individual whose system is out of balance and who therefore loses his ability to persist under even minor stresses, with rapid exhaustion caused by inner tension (the rejected green).

Again, in the following example:

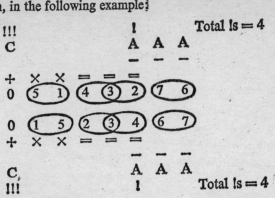

we have the work-group together in both 1st and 2nd selections, but it lies in the 'indifferent' area in both. There is conflict and anxiety, but in such a case as this, it could well be the result of his present situation or type of occupation, which evidently allow no scope for his capabilities. His ability to work is in abeyance because the circumstances are inappropriate; given different circumstances or more suitable work it is probable that the work-group would surge to the front and the present conflict disappear altogether. This is not a case of exhaustibility.

Exhaustibility makes itself apparent in the test by a deterioration of the unity of the work-group from first to second selection, and particularly by a pronounced movement towards the rear of one or more of the three work-group colours, especially the red and the green. Where the green recedes, it is persistence which falters, the mental tenacity to continue becoming readily exhausted; when the red recedes the exhaustion is likely to be more physical and indicates energy depletion. Recession of yellow implies a falling off in satisfaction or pleasure in the task – a sort of psychic exhaustion, but since it is less tangible and serious in its effects, it has less significance than either green or red.

CHAPTER SIX

THE MEANING
OF THE EIGHT COLOURS

Each of the eight colours has been carefully chosen because of its particular psychological and physiological meaning – its 'structure'. This meaning is of universal significance and is the same the world over, to young and old alike, to men and to women, to the educated and the backward, to the 'civilized' and the 'uncivilized'. In fact, the only limitation which can be placed on the general applicability of the test is the necessity to communicate to the person being tested; if he can understand what is required of him, see the colour-panels (whether or not he is colour-blind) and state his preferences, then the test applies to him.

Many people are antipathetically disposed towards 'psychological tests', especially to those which require the answering of numerous time-consuming questions or the sorting of a plethora of cards. In the experience of those administering the Lüscher Test this antipathy is very rarely encountered; the test is attractive and appealing to do, takes very little time and, in any event, those undertaking the test 'do not see how they can give anything away by picking colours!' It might well be that they would be less willing had they any idea of how revelatory the test actually is.

In this chapter, the meanings and significances of each of the eight colours is set out in some detail to enable the user to amplify the interpretations given in the Tables.

Grey (0)

The grey of the test is neither coloured, nor dark, nor light, and is entirely free from any stimulus or psychological tendency. It is neutral, neither subject nor object, neither inner nor outer, neither tension nor relaxation. Grey is not an occupied territory but a border; a border as a no-man's-land, as a demilitarized zone, a region of separation providing a partition between contrasting areas. Grey is a Berlin Wall, an Iron Curtain, on either side of which is a different approach.

Whoever chooses grey in the 1st position wants to wall everything off, to remain uncommitted and uninvolved so that he can shield himself from any outside influence or stimulus. He is unwilling to take part and insulates himself from direct participation by dealing with what he must mechanically and artificially. Even when apparently participating to the full, the person who selects grey first is really only participating by remote control, as it were – he stands aside and watches himself go through the motions, but he does not really allow himself to become involved. In this position, grey is entirely compensatory and is an attempt to ameliorate by non-involvement the circumstances resulting from the anxiety represented by the rejected colour(s).

Grey, with its special attribute of non-involvement, of 'having nothing to do with', contains a pronounced element of concealment. Where grey forms part of a group of two colours, for example, and occupies the 1st position, then what is wanted is non-involvement first and foremost, followed by an unadmitted and possibly unrecognized desire for what is represented by the colour in 2nd position.

On the other hand, the person who chooses grey in the last (8th) position wants to encompass everything – he rejects non-involvement – and feels that he has a perfect right to take part in anything which is going on around him, with the result that others may find him meddlesome, overinquisitive or intrusive. He finds the neutrality of grey boring and rejects its lifeless calm to the last place in the row. All the other effect-laden colours with their contrasting tensions and stimuli are preferred because they imply a greater degree of experience and interest. Whoever rejects grey, therefore, commits himself to things by his own readiness to be stimulated and by his anxiety not to miss out on anything. He wants to exhaust every possibility on his way to his goal and cannot let himself rest or be at peace until he has reached it.

Whoever chooses grey in 2nd position divides his world, on the one hand, into the compensatory and exaggerated area represented by the colour he has placed in the 1st position and, on the other hand, into all the remaining potentialities represented by the colours he is warding off or repressing out of the anxiety that he might become involved with them. The colour preceding a grey in the 2nd position represents the only mechanism through which he is willing to experience. Otherwise he is 'switched off' and insulated from the world around him. This does not mean that he will necessarily appear inactive or non-participating to others – on the contrary, he may appear to be very active as the compensation includes the endeavour to make up for his own inner feeling of meaninglessness, and for his own inability to act as the outcome of direct experience.

Even with grey in 3rd place, the lack of balance between the favoured colours preceding it and the colours which follow after the grey is still so charged with tension that the colours in the 1st and 2nd positions must be interpreted as compensations, and therefore as compulsive substitutes for some existing deficiency and for the anxiety which arises from it. For example, if the first three colours are 3 4 0, then a 'switching off' has taken place and the group 3 4 (red/ yellow) represents the compensatory method which has to be used in order to experience: in this case, 'expansive activity'. He *must* keep trying to expand his fields of action and experience in order to convince himself that *something* is running, as he himself is already out of the hunt, cut off and rather lost; nothing has much real meaning to him and he is no longer sure that he wants anything to mean a great deal. However, *he does not know all this*, and is usually most unwilling to let himself discover it; if he became aware of it, everything would tend to fall to pieces round him and it is for this reason that he *must* have the compensation. It is his hold on reality.

Grey in the first three places therefore contains a strong element of self-deception, especially since the compensation is often powerful and often appears very effective. Many leading figures in industry and commerce have compensations of this nature followed immediately by the concealing grey: this bears out 'a widely-held psychological theory that those who excel or stand out from their fellows do so less out of their own natural superiority than out of a compelling urge to escape something which causes anxiety and discontent'.*

Colours which appear now in front and now behind the grey, from first to second selection on repetition of the test, are indicative of an existing state of stress. Such 'grey-accompanying' colours are themselves conflict-laden so long as the grey occurs in the first half of the test (positions 1 to 4).

The average statistical position of grey is in 6th place, while it can transfer to 5th or 7th without being significant. In all other positions it is meaningful. In conditions of exhaustion, depletion or special stress (as, for example, just before an examination) grey tends to push further towards the front.

Blue (1)

The dark-blue of the test represents complete calm. Contemplation of this colour has a pacifying effect on the central

* I. Scott. *Making the Most of Manpower*: Lüscher Personnel Services, London, (1967).

nervous system. Blood pressure, pulse and respiration rate are all reduced, while self-protective mechanisms work to recharge the organism. The body adjusts itself to relaxation and recuperation, so that in sickness and exhaustion the need for this colour increases. Psychologically, the tendency to be sensitive and easily hurt also increases.

Dark-blue, like all four of the basic colours, is a chromatic representation of a basic biological need – physiologically, tranquillity; psychologically, contentment, contentment being peace plus gratification. Anyone in a situation as balanced, harmonious and tension-free as this feels settled, united and secure. Thus, blue represents the bonds one draws around oneself, unification and the sense of belonging. 'Blue is loyalty,' as they say, but where one's allies are concerned one is especially vulnerable, so blue corresponds to depth of feeling. Blue, as a relaxed sensitivity, is a prerequisite for empathy, for aesthetic experience and for meditative awareness.

Schelling uses pure-blue symbolism in his *Philosophy of Art* when he says: 'silence is the proper condition of beauty, like the calm of the untroubled sea'. Blue corresponds symbolically to calm water, to the quiet temperament, to femininity, to the illumination in the manuscript. Its sensory perception is sweetness, its emotional content is tenderness and its organ is the skin. Thus, eczema and acne can often be associated with disturbed relationships which involve (or should involve) tenderness, love or close affection, such as the family, young love and marriage.

Derived from the Sanskrit, the Pali word *Nila* has been given to the special dark-blue colour advised as the most suitable environment for the purposes of meditation. The German word for the basic biological mood represented by dark-blue is *Gemüt*. There is no English equivalent conveying exactly the same meaning, but 'sensitivity of feeling' comes close.

Dark-blue has considerable depth and fullness – it is

especially favoured by the overweight – and represents contentment and fulfilment. It is the blissful fulfilment of the highest ideals of unity, of at-one-ness, a reunion with Gaea, the Earth Mother. It is truth and trust, love and dedication, surrender and devotion. Blue is the timelessness of eternity, representing tradition and lasting values, and so tends to perpetuate the past.

When blue is chosen in 1st position, there is a need either for emotional tranquillity, peace, harmony and contentment or there is a physiological need for rest, relaxation and an opportunity to recuperate. Whoever favours blue wants a calm and orderly environment, free from upsets and disturbance, in which events move and develop smoothly, along more or less traditional lines; an environment in which his relationships with others are placid and free from contention. When the 1st-position blue is chosen purely for itself and not as a compensation, then it implies a quietness of spirit, calmness of manner and a concern that the business of living shall be dealt with ethically and with integrity – there is a need for him to feel that he can trust and be trusted by his associates and those close to him.

When blue is chosen in the 6th, 7th or 8th positions, however, this need for equanimity and for mutual trust in his relationships remains unsatisfied, giving rise to an anxiety which is greater the farther back in the row the colour is placed. Existing emotional relationships or his professional associations are being rejected because they do not measure up to his high standards of what is required of them and are found to be either boring or restrictive. He finds them burdensome, disheartening and oppressive, a tie from which he would like to escape. He may actually do this, by leaving his home or changing his job, but where he considers his responsibilities are such that he cannot actually sever his connexion with them, he will still be inclined to escape mentally into some compensatory activity. Thus, rejected dark-blue means: severance of ties (or, at least, the wish to sever them) and results in restless or inconstant behaviour and a degree of mental agitation. The ability to concentrate may suffer as a result, and in children this is liable to take the form of difficulty in learning. In adults the resulting tension, if long continued, can lead to disturbances of the nervous system involving the heart and the circulation as a result of cardio-vascular changes.

Rejected dark-blue, as an unsatisfied need for emotional fulfilment, may give rise to a compensatory preference for green. In this case the green insistence on the self implies a proud and rebellious demand for independence, often found in youngsters who want to break loose from family and parental apron-strings.

Frequently, rejected dark-blue gives rise to a preference for red as a compensation, this implying a desire for stimuli. When an unsatisfied need for emotional fulfilment is accompanied by a compensatory red as the *modus operandi* in 1st position, then an attempt is being made to dull this feeling of non-fulfilment by impassioned behaviour or by sexuality – the Don Juan syndrome. Where sexual promiscuity is repudiated as an acceptable substitute for a rejected dark-blue, then the red compensation will probably take the form of vigorous or adventurous activity in which the individual pits himself against the dangers of some exciting pursuit, such as driving racing automobiles or hunting big game.

Often yellow is chosen in the attempt to compensate for a rejected blue. Yellow means: the search for a way out of difficulties. In this case, the oppressive lack of emotional fulfilment demands that the situation be eased and the associated depression lifted, so there is a restless search for some solution. This search may be not only for a solution to an existing condition of emotional vulnerability, but may go beyond it into a search for some more satisfying state of spiritual accord, such as philosophical or metaphysical understanding, preoccupation with religious teachings, an interest in furthering movements devoted to bringing about universal brotherhood, and so forth.

Statistically, blue is of special significance if it does not stand somewhere in the first four positions.

Green (2)

The green of the test contains a certain amount of blue and is the test-colour representing the physiological condition of 'elastic tension'. It expresses itself psychologically as the will in operation, as perseverance and tenacity. Blue-green is therefore an expression of firmness, of constancy and, above all, of resistance to change. It indicates constancy of viewpoint as well as constant self-awareness and places a high value on the 'I' in all forms of possession and self-affirmation, since possession is regarded as increasing both security and self-esteem. From this, we can see that the person who chooses green in the 1st position wants to increase his certainty in his own value, either by self-assertiveness, by holding fast to some idealized picture he has of himself, or by the acknowledgement he expects from others in deference to his possessions – whether because of his greater wealth or in terms of his superiority in physical, educational or cultural attainments.

Green corresponds symbolically to the majestic sequoia, deep-rooted, proud and unchanging, towering over lesser trees, to the austere and autocratic temperament, to the tension in the bow-string. Its sensory perception is astringence, its emotional content is pride, and its organs are the smooth (involuntary) muscles. Thus gastric ulcers and digestive upsets are often associated with worry over possible loss of standing or personal failure.

Green as tension therefore acts as a dam behind which the excitation of external stimuli builds up without being released, increasing the sense of pride, of self-controlled superiority to others, of power, of being in control of events, or at least of being able to manage and direct them. This damming-up and suppression of external stimuli lead to many forms and degrees of 'control', not only in the sense of directed drives, but also as detailed accuracy in checking and verifying facts, as precise and accurate memory, as clarity of presentation, critical analysis and logical consistency – all the way up to abstract formalism. This 'green' behaviour can also find expression in a quest for better conditions, such as improved health, or a longer or more useful life both for himself and for others. In this case we have the reformer, bent on ameliorating conditions.

But, above all, the person who chooses green wants his own opinions to prevail, to feel himself justified as a representative of basic and immutable principles. As a result, he puts himself on a pedestal and tends to moralize to and lecture others.

Whoever chooses green in the 1st position wishes to impress. He needs to be recognized, to hold his own and to have his own way against opposition and resistance. The person who chooses green in 6th, 7th or 8th positions wants the same things, but has been weakened by the resistance he has encountered and feels reduced in stature by the lack of recognition. This leads to tension and to distress because of the imperative nature of his desires and possibly also from actual physical weakness. This distress makes itself felt as a tangible resistance, an actual physical pressure (as, for example, in chest or heart complaints), or as hardship or coercion – all of which he seeks to avoid. The farther back in the row the green, the more urgently he seeks to avoid this sense of pressure.

Rejected green therefore means: 'anxiety to liberate himself from the tensions imposed by non-recognition'. Loss of his own powers of resistance and tenacity, anxiety over possible loss of standing or position, as well as the reduction in his ability to assert himself, all combine to produce such concern over his own possible failure as an individual that he is likely to put all the blame onto others and adopt a critical, caustic and derogatory attitude towards them. While green in 1st position *can* mean a stubborn and self-opinionated attitude, when green is rejected it always does.

Rejected green is often compensated for by putting blue in 1st position because it is hoped that this will lead to peace and freedom from tension. People who make this selection are looking for a peaceful haven where they can find contentment and no longer have to make the intolerable effort required to assert their position.

Sometimes rejected green is compensated by red in 1st position. Red means the desire for excitation and stimulus, and since rejected green itself expresses an irritating state of tension leading to impatience and loss of self-control, this combination results in considerable impetuosity, uncontrollable outbursts of temper, hypertension and cardiovascular changes. These can bring about incoherence, partial loss of consciousness or even apoplectic seizures.

Occasionally an attempt is made to compensate for the intolerable tension of a rejected green by selecting yellow in 1st position as a way out of the difficulty. This 'flight to freedom' is an attempt to escape the feeling of constriction, the pressure which causes it and the possible breakdown in health which may follow. Such a compensation is rarely adequate, consisting as it does in efforts to divert the attention by travel, visiting new places, taking up new hobbies and so forth.

Green is significant when it does not appear in the 2nd, 3rd or 4th positions.

Red (3)

The red of the test, with its admixture of yellow giving it an orange hue, represents an energy-expending physiological condition. It speeds up the pulse, raises blood pressure and increases the respiration rate. Red is the expression of vital force, of nervous and glandular activity, and so it has the meaning of *desire* and of all forms of appetite and craving. Red is the urge to achieve results, to win success; it is hungrily to desire all those things which offer intensity of living and fullness of experience. Red is impulse, the will-to-win, and all forms of vitality and power from sexual potency to revolutionary transformation. It is the impulse towards active doing, towards sport, struggle, competition, eroticism and enterprising productivity. Red is 'impact of the will' or 'force of will' as distinct from the green 'elasticity of the will'.

Red corresponds symbolically to the blood of conquest, to the Pentecostal flame igniting the human spirit, to the sanguine temperament and to masculinity. Its sensory perception is appetite, its emotional content is desire, and its organs are the striated (voluntary) muscles, the sympathetic nervous system and the organs of reproduction. Thus, physical and nervous exhaustion, heart disorders and loss either of potency or of sexual desire are often to be seen accompanying a rejected red. In temporal terms, red is the present.

Whoever chooses red in the 1st position wants his own activities to bring him intensity of experience and fullness of living. What form these activities will take – cooperative enterprise, leadership, creative endeavour, development and expansion, eroticism, sensual pursuit of physical appetite, or over-dramatic and exaggerated activity – will be indicated in the main by the colour which accompanies red in the group.

Sexually, red standing by itself in the 1st position (as a normal +, not as a compensation) suggests a more or less controlled sexual drive, with the possibility of occasional outbreaks of impulsive sexual experience: the reasonably faithful partner who may sometimes yield to temptation without it necessarily meaning very much. However, if red is compensatory in the 1st position, the sexual drive is not only powerful but the ability to satisfy it is inhibited by the egocentricity which compulsively demands conquest with variety of experience and sensation, leading to sexual experimentation, promiscuity and frequent infidelities. In extreme cases, this can include the nymphomaniac and the satyr, neither of whom ever achieve real satisfaction or release from tension through the sexual act. When red is part of the × group, sexuality is more restrained and there is the desire to restrict sexual intercourse to a partner who complies with the characteristics personified by the + group. With red in the 'indifferent' area (= group), sexuality is becoming inhibited, and when red is rejected, sexual desire has either largely disappeared, is being rigorously suppressed, or impotence or frigidity have set in.

Rejected red in 6th, 7th or 8th positions implies that its stimulating intensity is regarded as antagonistic. Whoever rejects red is already in a state of over-stimulation, readily becoming irritated either because he is suffering from a lack of vitality (as, for example, through physical exhaustion or cardiac insufficiency), or because he feels beset by well-nigh insoluble problems. He feels his environment to be dangerous and out of his control; in these circumstances the colour appears to him not in its special significance of power and strength, but as something menacing. Rejected red therefore means: 'seeks protection from anything which might excite, aggravate or weaken further', and this desire for protection is, of course, the more intense the closer red is to the 8th position.

Usually blue is chosen in 1st position as the compensation for rejected red because a peaceful environment is needed as a 'tranquillizer'. With this blue combination there is often a masochistic clinging to a sexual partner accompanied by the feeling of being unloved and unappreciated. Physiologically, this combination of rejected red and compensatory blue is often seen in those suffering from the frustrations and anxieties of the business world and in executives heading for heart disease (for which it provides an excellent early warning). Presidents, vice-presidents and others with this combination need a vacation, a medical check-up and an opportunity to reassemble their physical resources.

Rejected red and preferred green are seldom found, because in such a condition of helplessness it is only possible to contain the situation for a short while with 'green' resilience. However, this choice does sometimes occur when an individual is trying to overcome nervous and physical exhaustion by will power alone.

More frequently, yellow is found in 1st position as a compensation for the debilitating effects of rejected red and means 'a search for a way out'. But this choice is also usually of short duration as it yields a picture of despair.

Red is significant if it does not stand in the first three positions.

Yellow

Yellow is the brightest colour in the test and its effect is light and cheerful. Because red appears denser and heavier than yellow it is stimulative; because yellow is lighter and less dense than red it is more suggestive than stimulative. For instance, while yellow increases blood pressure, pulse and respiration rates in a manner similar to red, yet it is noticeably less stable in the way in which it does so. Yellow's principal characteristics are its brightness, its reflectivity, its radiant quality and its non-substantial cheerfulness. Yellow expresses uninhibited expansiveness, a loosening or relaxation. As opposed to green (2) in which tension-induced contraction can even result in cramp or spasm, yellow represents relaxation and dilatation. Psychologically, relaxation means release from burdens, problems, harassment or restriction.

Yellow corresponds symbolically to the welcoming warmth of sunlight, to the aspirational halo round the Holy Grail, to the cheerful spirit and to happiness. Its sensory perception is piquancy, its emotional content is hopeful volatility, and its organs are the sympathetic and parasympathetic nervous systems. Unlike red, which also acts on these systems, yellow activity is more uncertain and tends to lack red's coherence and design. The 'yellow' individual may be a whirlwind of industry, but his industriousness comes in fits and starts.

If yellow is chosen in 1st place, it shows the desire for release and the hope or expectation of greater happiness, and implies some minor or major conflict from which release is needed. This hope of happiness, in all its countless forms from sexual adventure to philosophies offering enlightenment and perfection, is always directed towards the future; yellow presses forward, towards the new, the modern, the developing and the unformed.

Where yellow is heavily emphasized and compensatory, there is not only a strong desire to escape from existing difficulties, by finding a way out which will bring release, but there is also likely to be superficiality, change for the sake of change and an eager quest for alternative experience. Like green, yellow wants to achieve importance and the high regard of others but, unlike green, which is proud and self-contained, yellow is never at rest, straining ever outwards in its pursuits of its ambitions. Where yellow is compulsive it can therefore fall into the trap of envy (the 'green eye of the little yellow god').

Green is persistence, yellow is change. Green is tension, yellow is relaxation. Between these poles there is a conflict which arises out of their incompatibility. Here 'green' ambition, self-insistence and demand for prestige are at war with yellow's hopeful pursuit of happy experience and adventure. Where green predominates, the involuntary muscles are chronically under strain, with the result that pathological disturbances may occur in the stomach or intestines, or in the heart and circulatory systems – conditions often lying in wait for the over-ambitious. Since the degree of tension is often intolerable where such conditions exist, the green is usually rejected and yellow favoured in the attempt to compensate for and relax this tension.

If yellow is rejected and placed in 6th, 7th or 8th position, then hopes have been disappointed, the individual is confronting emptiness and feels isolated or cut off from others. In so serious a mood the brightness and insubstantial quality of yellow are regarded as inappropriate and superficial, the greater the disappointment the farther back in the row the yellow being placed. Rejected yellow implies that turmoil has resulted from disappointment and from the feeling that hopes are not going to be realized. This turmoil may take the form of irritability, discouragement or mistrust and suspicion of others and of their intentions. If we consider how many people achieve and maintain their interest in life solely from their hopes and expectations, it will be appreciated how devastating is the effect of hopelessness, and that rejected yellow reveals an alarming deprivation of many aspects of life. Rejected yellow therefore means: 'is attempting to protect himself against isolation and further loss or disappointment'.

Compensations take various forms. Frequently blue is chosen in the 1st position, showing that peace and unity are needed as a means of achieving a measure of content. Rejected yellow and preferred blue reflect the tendency to cling, to hang on to the familiar; this combination is common and reveals itself in a rather masochistic type of attachment.

An attempt can also be made to compensate for hopelessness by striving for security, position and prestige. In this case, green will be the essential method of position 1.

If red occurs in 1st position, then the pursuit of adventure, of intense experience – especially sexual excess – will be the means adopted to escape the sense of disappointment and isolation.

Yellow is significant if it does not occur in the 2nd to 5th positions.

Violet (5)

Violet is a mixture of red and blue and, though a separate and distinct colour, manages to retain something of the properties of both as a red-blue amalgamation, despite losing the clarity of purpose of the two colours. Violet attempts to unify the impulsive conquest of red and the gentle surrender of blue, becoming representative of 'identification'. This identification is a sort of mystic union, a high degree of sensitive intimacy leading to complete fusion between subject and object, so that everything which is thought and desired must become Reality. In a way, this is enchantment, a dream made fact, a magical state in which wishes are fulfilled – so the person who prefers violet wants to achieve a 'magical' relationship. He not only wants to be beglamoured himself, but at the same time he wants to charm and delight others, to exert a degree of fascination over them because, although this is a magical identification, the distinction between subject and object still exists.

Violet can mean identification as an intimate, erotic blending, or it can lead to an intuitive and sensitive understanding. But its somewhat unreal and wish-fulfillment quality can also mean identification as an inability to differentiate or as an irresolute wavering, either of which may result in irresponsibility.

The mentally mature will normally prefer one of the basic colours rather than violet; the mentally and emotionally immature on the other hand, may prefer violet. In the case of 1,600 pre-adolescent schoolchildren, 75% of them preferred violet. Statistics embracing Iranians, Africans and

Brazilian Indians showed a marked preference for this colour as compared with Euro-Caucasians. Erbsloeh's investigations have shown that glandular and hormonal activity during pregnancy tend to result in a preference for violet and that this is also often the case when thyroid malfunction exists. Hyper-thyroidism (when psychosomatic and not the result of iodine deficiency) is a condition resulting from long-sustained stress, shock or conditions in early life subjecting sufferers to undue fear or terror, their emotions being very unstably under their control. They need a special understanding, gentle treatment and a tenderness which can pacify their fears. Exactly the same thing can very often be said of women during pregnancy, many of whom become emotionally insecure at this time.

The preference for violet among pre-adolescents highlights the fact that, to them, the world is still a magical place in which they have only to rub Aladdin's lamp for its slave to bring them what they want – an attitude which certainly has its points, but which it is probably inadvisable to carry over into adult life.

The homosexual and the lesbian often show their own emotional insecurity by a preference for violet as a compensation. Here we have the case of people whose emotional fears lead them to try to create around themselves a fairyland in which they can consider the rest of the world well lost so long as they have each other. However, while a significant proportion of homosexuals of both sexes have violet in 1st place, it should not be assumed that a preference for violet necessarily implies homosexual practice nor even homosexual leanings.

When violet occurs in 1st position it is therefore necessary to investigate a little further and discover which violet attribute is indicated. Is it a pre-adolescent immaturity carried forward into adult life? In this event, the person will tend to be unrealistic and have difficulty in distinguishing the practical from the visionary. Is there glandular malfunction or some other condition leading to emotional insecurity? If so, then the person will have a special need for sensitive understanding from a partner with whom he or she can identify. If neither of these is the case, then the person wishes to be approved of for his charm and fascination, for his delightful manners and his winning ways – he wants to cast a spell on others. He is sensitive and appreciative, but does not want his relationships to involve him in excessive responsibility.

When violet occurs in 8th position, the desire for a mystic intimacy with another has been rejected or suppressed because of the apparent impossibility of it being fulfilled or because conditions are entirely unsuitable. This results in a rather critical reserve and an unwillingness to commit oneself at all deeply to any relationship, either personal or professional, until one knows exactly where one stands and can see what the responsibilities of this relationship will involve. At the same time, the need for identification and intuitive understanding which are implied by violet are projected onto objects rather than people, giving rise to aesthetic appreciation, the ability to arrive at one's own independent judgement and an increased leaning towards occupations of a professional or scientific nature.

Violet is not significant if it falls in 3rd to 7th places, nor – in the case of pregnancy or pre-adolescence – in 1st and 2nd places.

Brown (6)

The brown of the test is a darkened yellow-red. The impulsive vitality of red is reduced, dampened and rendered more peaceful through this darkening – it is 'broken-down' as the painter would put it. Brown has therefore forfeited the expansive creative impulse, the active vital force of red. Vitality is no longer actively effective, but passively receptive and sensory.

Brown therefore represents sensation as it applies to the bodily senses. It is sensuous, relating directly to the physical body, and its position in the row gives an indication of the body's sensory condition. If brown, for example, is in the 'indifferent' area (where statistically it occurs most frequently) then the sensory state and physical condition of the body are not being given undue weight. This is as it should be, since a healthy and contented body should obtrude little on its owner's attention. Where there is physical discomfort or *dis-ease*, then brown begins to move towards the beginning of the row, demonstrating the greater emphasis which is being placed on physical unease and the greater need for conditions which will allow this discomfort to be ameliorated.

The dispossessed and the rootless, having no hearth of their own before which they can relax and be at ease, and with little prospect of security and physical contentment ahead of them, are often found to place brown right at the beginning of the row. This was particularly the case amongst those who became displaced persons as a result of World War II. It was not that their bodies were necessarily more physically sensitive, but that there was no place where they could feel secure and where they could enjoy those creature comforts with which the more fortunate are able to surround themselves. So brown also indicates the importance placed on 'roots': on hearth, home and the company of one's own kind, on gregarious and familial security.

If brown stands in the first half of the row, and especially in the first two places, there exists an increased need for physical ease and sensuous contentment, for release from some situation which is bringing about a feeling of discomfort. This situation may be one of insecurity, of actual physical illness; it may be an atmosphere of conflict, or the existence of problems with which the individual feels unable to cope. Whatever the cause, the sensory condition of the body is being adversely affected, greater emphasis being placed on the need to provide a safer environment for it.

Where brown is placed in 8th position, this need for relaxed ease is rejected altogether. Here physical comfort and sensory satisfaction are interpreted as weaknesses to be overcome. The rejector of brown considers he is made of sterner stuff and wishes to stand out as an individualist. Not for him the gregariousness or inter-dependency of brown, nor any pandering to the wants of his body. This suppression of the ability to enjoy physical sensation, however, may easily lead to an anxiety-producing deficit demanding some form of compensation – including the possibility of compulsive sexual activity – in the endeavour to experience some of the physical sensation which is being over-rigorously suppressed.

Brown is significant if it does not stand in the 5th to 7th positions.

Black (7)

Black is the darkest colour and is, in fact, the negation of colour itself. Black represents the absolute boundary beyond which life ceases, and so expresses the idea of nothingness, of extinction. Black is the 'No' as opposed to the 'Yes' of white. White is the virgin page on which the story has yet to be written, black is the end beyond which there is nothing more. While white is included in the Full Lüscher Test, it does not occur in the eight colours, but white and black are the two extremes, the Alpha and the Omega, the beginning and the end. In the Eight-colour Test, the nearest approach to white is the bright yellow, and if black and yellow are found together in a group, then 'extreme' behaviour of one sort or another is indicated.

Black, as negation itself, represents renunciation, the ultimate surrender or relinquishment, and has a strong effect on any colour which occurs in the same group, emphasizing and enforcing the characteristic of that colour.

If black occurs in the first half of the test, and especially in the first three places, it results in compensatory behaviour of an extreme nature. Whoever chooses black in the 1st position wants to renounce everything out of a stubborn protest against the existing state in which he feels that nothing is as it should be. He is in revolt against Fate, or at least against his own fate, and is liable to act precipitately and unwisely in this revolt.

With black in 2nd place, he believes himself willing to renounce everything else providing he can have whatever is represented by the colour he put in position 1. If, for example, red is in 1st place with black in 2nd, then the satisfaction of exaggerated desires is expected to compensate for all that is deficient. With blue preceding black, then absolute tranquillity is expected to restore disturbed harmony and emotional unrest. With yellow preceding black in the first two positions, some abrupt and possibly catastrophic action or change of course is expected to put an end to his troubles. With grey and black, then the protection of total non-involvement will help to overcome general intolerability.

Black in the 3rd position demands the compensation afforded by the colours in the first two places. And, as in the case of grey, colours which appear before the black on the first selection and after it on the second selection, when they occur in the first half of the test, are similarly conflict-laden and indicate an additional source of anxiety.

Black in the 8th position is statistically in its most frequent position, representing a more or less normal desire not to have to relinquish anything, and to be in control of one's own actions and decisions. When this position is one of anxiety, however, to lose or be deprived of anything becomes a matter of conflict and, since the individual finds it most distressing to have to relinquish, he runs the danger of demanding too much.

CHAPTER SEVEN

STRUCTURAL MEANING
OF THE COLOUR PAIRS

Each group of two colours has a structural meaning of its own which is independent of its position in the row. The *functional* interpretation of the corresponding attitude or characteristic naturally varies, depending on whether a +, ×, = or − group is involved.

While a group may consist of a single colour (in which case its structural meaning is as already given in the last chapter), yet most of the groups encountered will be in pairs of two colours; of these there are 56. A brief description of these 56 structural groups is given here to help towards a fuller understanding of the basis on which the more comprehensive interpretations of the Tables are developed.

It will be found that there is an apparent duplication of these 'group-meanings'; for example, both 0 3 (grey/red) and 3 0 (red/grey) have the meaning of 'Impulsiveness', but the manner in which this impulsiveness is demonstrated is not quite the same for one as it is for the other. This applies also to many of the other pairs, each of which can occur in either order.

The function symbol (+, ×, = or −, but *not* + −) will naturally affect the interpretation to be attached to the structural group-meaning. If we call this group-meaning 'M', then:

Group marked + means 'Wants to be or to have "M".'
or 'Must be or must have "M".'
Group marked × means 'Is being "M" or feels in an "M" situation.'
or '"M" behaviour is the most appropriate.'
Group marked = means '"M" behaviour is inappropriate at present.'
or '"M" is in reserve or under restraint.'
Group marked − means 'Does not want to be or to have "M".'
or 'Feels unable to be or to have "M".'

Thus, using the group 0 3 (grey/red) as an example:

0 3 Wants to be free to follow his impulses and act
+ + as the spirit moves him.

0 3
× × Acts on impulse.

0 3 Impulsiveness is inappropriate to the situation, or
= = impulsiveness is being kept under control (or both).

0 3 Dislikes impulsive action (in himself and in
− − others).

The short descriptions which follow the structural meanings of the colour pairs have been worded in most cases to correspond with the + function. These would require the same modification as the structural meaning itself to make them applicable to the remaining functions.

0 1

Grey/Blue

Structural meaning: 'An Interval of Tranquillity'
or   'A Period of Recuperation'

The protective shield of grey (0) precedes the need for peace (1) and therefore non-involvement takes precedence over tranquillity. Remaining uncommitted is expected to bring peace in its train.

0 2

Grey/Green

Structural meaning: 'Separative Self-Insistence'
or   'Defensive Superiority'

The need for protection precedes the egocentric green, implying extreme caution in preserving interests and position. The self-regarding quality of green is associated also with a sense of superiority, the grey insulation implying unwillingness to undermine this self-esteem by too close contact with others. Since the grey comes first, this characteristic tends to be concealed or covert in its application.

0 3

Grey/Red

Structural meaning: 'Impulsiveness'
or   'Ill-Considered Action'

With the protective and concealing grey preceding the active red, impulsive action tends to be of a rather covert nature, carried out with the hope of being neither committed nor involved in consequences.

0 4

Grey/Yellow

Structural meaning: 'Indecision'
or   'Lack of Resolution'

Here it is hope, aspiration and the solution to problems (4) which lie behind the concealing wall of grey (0) and are therefore lost in fog, as it were. This implies an irresolute groping for the right solution, or even the right thing to hope for or aspire to. Further, making a definite decision would mean committing oneself to a course of action extending into the future.

0 5

Grey/Violet

Structural meaning: 'Cautious Sensitivity'
or 'Tentative Identification'
The desire to be identified with someone or
something exists but must not be allowed to
appear openly, so all approaches are made
tentatively and with caution.

0 6

Grey/Brown

Structural meaning: 'Exhaustion'
or 'Depletion'
Here protection for the body and its sensory
condition is involved. To avoid being caught
up in any problem or disturbance may afford
the constitution the opportunity to recover.

0 7

Grey/Black

Structural meaning: 'Separative Isolation'
or 'Total Non-Involvement'
Here non-involvement is exaggerated and
enforced by the imperative nature of black,
while everything which follows in the sequence
is renounced and considered unimportant.

1 0

Blue/Grey

Structural meaning: 'An Interval of
Tranquillity'
or 'A Period of
Recuperation'
Protection from the stresses imposed by the
colours following the grey will be afforded if
peaceful conditions can be obtained.

1 2

Blue/Green

Structural meaning: 'Discriminating Control'
or 'Self-Contained
Orderliness'
Sensitivity and accurate understanding lead
to an increase in self-esteem, encouraging
order and method. Precision and exactitude
bordering on the fussy and over-solicitous may
result. Both colours are autocentric, making for
self-containment.

1 3

Blue/Red

Structural meaning: 'Cooperative
Enterprise'
     or   'Emotional Fulfilment'
In the outside or working life, implies the ability
to get along with one's associates, to cooper-
ate with them to mutual benefit and to the
benefit of the organization. In the private or
domestic life, implies a harmonious combination of sexual activity and tenderness. In both,
the fact that blue precedes red indicates that
greater importance is placed on harmony and
cooperation than on activity. Cooperation and
understanding, it is assumed, will lead to more
creative action.

1 4

Blue/Yellow

Structural meaning: 'Emotional
Dependency'
     or   'Group-Oriented
Helpfulness'
The blue desire to understand and be under-
stood and yellow aspiration lead to behaviour
designed to attract the affection of others.
Both colours are heteronomous, making this
an 'other-determined' group.

1 5

Blue/Violet

Structural meaning: 'Aesthetic Susceptibility'
     or   'Erotic Sensitivity'
Peace and fulfilment are here to be achieved
through some form of fascination, either by
absorbtion with the beautiful and the aesthetic,
or by the pursuit of some idealized relationship.

1 6

Blue/Brown

Structural meaning: 'Sensual Ease'
     or   'Indolent Attachment'
Peace and security can here only be achieved
by relieving the condition of physical unease
and being treated with social consideration.

17

Blue/Black

Structural meaning: 'Absolute Peace'
Black following blue enforces as imperative the blue need for tranquillity and implies renunciation of all that is represented by the colours following black. Where this group occurs towards one end of the row with 3 4 (or 4 3) towards the other, instability of the self-regulating nervous system should be suspected.

20

Green/Grey

Structural meaning: 'Separative
                                    Self-Insistence'
            or   'Defensive Superiority'
Here the defensiveness of green is emphasized and exaggerated by the defensive wall of grey. Self-esteem, the need to impress and prestige-consciousness are all magnified, while the attributes of the colours following the grey are minimized.

21

Green/Blue

Structural meaning: 'Discriminating Control'
            or   'Self-Contained
                                    Orderliness'
Precision, logic and the need to be proved right take precedence over the understanding blue, so that order and method are now more oriented towards the increase of self-esteem than in the group 1 2. Here control and orderliness may strike others as 'bossiness'. Both colours are concentric, making this a self-contained group.

23

Green/Red

Structural meaning: 'Purposeful Activity'
            or   'Controlled Initiative'
A determined and authoritative group, containing as it does both the autonomous colours. With green as the first colour, action (3) is designed to lead to greater authority and prestige for the self (2). Leadership, management and the exercise of control.

2 4

Green/Yellow

Structural meaning: 'Demand for
                              Appreciation'
              or   'Ambition'
Aspiration (4) is directed towards increased
esteem both in one's own eyes and in the eyes
of others (2). Ambitious self-interest or action
designed to bring about recognition from
others.

2 5

Green/Violet

Structural meaning: 'Flexible
                              Self-Insistence'
              or   'Irresponsible Charm'
Pleasantness of manner designed to win the
regard of others, but without committing oneself or assuming responsibility.

2 6

Green/Brown

Structural meaning: 'Demand for Physical
                              Relief'
              or   'Insistence on Comfort'
The self (2) can continue to maintain itself
only if conditions of unease (6) are relieved.

2 7

Green/Black

Structural meaning: 'Obstinate Exclusion'
              or   'Prejudiced
                              Self-Righteousness'
Here the green insistence on self, with its
tendency to consider itself right, is enforced
and made even more imperative by black. Any
attempt by others to exert influence is resolu-
tely shut out.

3 0

Red/Grey

Structural meaning: 'Impulsiveness'
              or   'Ill-Considered Action'
Action for its own sake, with insufficient
attention paid to consequences since these
are behind the concealing grey. Unlike 0 3,
there is little attempt to conceal the action
itself.

3 1

Red/Blue

Structural meaning: 'Cooperative
Enterprise'
or 'Emotional Fulfilment'

As for 1 3, except that here greater emphasis
is placed on activity than on cooperation and
harmony. Right activity, it is assumed, will lead
to harmony in any event.

3 2

Red/Green

Structural meaning: 'Purposeful Activity'
or 'Controlled Initiative'

As for 2 3, except that here action and the
exercise of one's own initiative are directed
more for the pleasure of exercising them than
for the high regard they may obtain from
others. Contains both the autonomous colours
and is therefore a 'self-determined' group.

3 4

Red/Yellow

Structural meaning: 'Expansive Activity'
or 'Development of New
Fields'

Both red and yellow being ex-centric, this is a
very outgoing and active group. Action (3)
for the sake of action and always directed
towards the new and undiscovered (4). Where
this group occurs towards one end of the row
with 1 7 (or 7 1) towards the other, instability of
the self-regulating nervous system should be
suspected.

3 5

Red/Violet

Structural meaning: 'Susceptibility to
Stimulus'
or 'Responsiveness'

Desires and actions (3) are directed towards
things which fascinate, stimulate and enthral
(5), while the actions themselves are designed
to fascinate others. Can be either erotic or
aesthetic.

3 6

Red/Brown

Structural meaning: 'Sensual Gratification'
or   'Self-Indulgence'
Here activity (3) is restricted by the fact that the body must not be disturbed or otherwise inconvenienced (6). Action is therefore aimed at gratifying the senses.

3 7

Red/Black

Structural meaning: 'Exaggerated Desire'
or   'Dramatization'
The normal desirousness of red is made compulsive and enforced by black.

4 0

Yellow/Grey

Structural meaning: 'Indecision'
or   'Lack of Resolution'
The need for a solution (4) predominates, but is walled off by grey and therefore separated from all other areas in which the solution might be found. Unlike 0 4, there is a willingness to be committed, but the grey barrier makes it difficult to discover just what one should commit oneself to.

4 1

Yellow/Blue

Structural meaning: 'Emotional Dependency'
or   'Group-Oriented
Helpfulness'
Both these colours are heteronomous, therefore the group is more effect than cause. The hope (4) is for affection and understanding (1), leading to activity designed to attract affection.

4 2

Yellow/Green

Structural meaning: 'Demand for
Appreciation'
or   'Ambition'
Less self-determined than 2 4 (*qv*). Here ambition is less a self-directed drive than a hope that by keeping alert and observant fresh avenues will open up and allow recognition to be achieved.

4 3

Yellow/Red

Structural meaning: 'Expansive Activity'
      or   'Development of New
               Fields'

The two brightest colours, both being ex-centric, make this a very outgoing and active group. The activity (3) is less controlled than in the group 3 4, since yellow (4) makes it both more superficial and more experimental, searching for something new and satisfying. Where this group occurs towards one end of the row with 1 7 (or 7 1) towards the other, instability of the self-regulating nervous system should be suspected.

4 5

Yellow/Violet

Structural meaning 'The Lure of Fantasy'
      or   'Thirst for Adventure'

Here hopes and aspirations (4) are expressed through fascination, imagination and fantasy (5), leading to a rather unreal thirst for adventure or vicarious experience.

4 6

Yellow/Brown

Structural meaning: 'Total Security'
      or   'Untrammelled Ease'

Here the solution (4) requires physical ease and freedom from any problems or fears of insecurity.

4 7

Yellow/Black

Structural meaning: 'Sudden Crisis'
      or   'Headstrong Decisions'

Here the two most extreme colours, the brightest and the darkest, are together, indicating that there can be no middle course, but only a 'Yes' or a 'No' answer. A solution (4) *must* be found (7), often by impetuous and headstrong means.

5 0

Violet/Grey

Structural meaning: 'Cautious Sensitivity'
      or   'Tentative Identification'
Sensitivity to atmosphere and environment
(5) accompanied by the desire to protect it
from any disturbing influence (0).

5 1

Violet/Blue

Structural meaning: 'Aesthetic
                    Susceptibility'
      or   'Erotic Sensitivity'
Differs from 1 5 in that emphasis is placed on
the idealized (and probably rather unreal)
condition of identification. Often found as a
compensation amongst those whose sexual
relationships are unorthodox but who have a
well-developed feeling for the beautiful and the
aesthetic.

5 2

Violet/Green

Structural meaning: 'Flexible
                    Self-Insistence'
      or   'Irresponsible Charm'
As for 2 5, but with greater emphasis on charm
and on the unwillingness to accept the responsibilities of close relationships.

5 3

Violet/Red

Structural meaning: 'Susceptibility to
                    Stimulus'
      or   'Responsiveness'
Fascinated by anything stimulating or exciting.
Similar to 3 5 but rather less responsible.

5 4

Violet/Yellow

Structural meaning: 'The Lure of Fantasy'
      or   'Thirst for Adventure'
The future must hold excitement, stimulation
and interest. Open in his charm, but over-
imaginative.

5 6

Violet/Brown

Structural meaning: 'Sensuousness'
or   'Voluptuousness'
Here the fascination (5) has to do with the
things which give the body pleasure (6), such
as good food, luxurious surroundings, fine
raiment and so forth.

5 7

Violet/Black

Structural meaning: 'Need for Identification'
or   'Compulsive Blending'
Here the desire to merge and identify (5) is
enforced and made compulsive by black (7).
Must form part of something or feel identified
with someone.

6 0

Brown/Grey

Structural meaning: 'Exhaustion'
or   'Depletion'
Here bodily ease and freedom from anything
which might cause physical or sensory distress are paramount. The body must be protected and allowed to recover. Similar to 0 6,
but there is greater emphasis on the need for
considerate treatment.

6 1

Brown/Blue

Structural meaning: 'Sensual Ease'
or   'Indolent Attachment'
As for 1 6, but with greater emphasis on the
physical need for gentle handling and considerate treatment.

6 2

Brown/Green

Structural meaning: 'Demand for Physical
Relief'
or   'Insistence on Comfort'
Here the body needs relief (6) but will power (2)
is being exerted to handle existing difficulties.
There is considerable strain involved and a
more relaxed environment is necessary.

6 3

Brown/Red

Structural meaning: 'Sensual Gratification'
or   'Self-Indulgence'
The bodily desire for conditions which gratify the senses (6) is followed immediately by the desirous red, emphasizing the drive towards self-gratification. A more self-indulgent group than 3 6.

6 4

Brown/Yellow

Structural meaning: 'Total Security'
or   'Untrammelled Ease'
Bodily relief (6) is preferred even to hopes for the future (4), resulting in surrender to a static and problem-free existence making minimal demands.

6 5

Brown/Violet

Structural meaning: 'Sensuousness'
or   'Voluptuousness'
As for 5 6, but with more emphasis on the physical senses.

6 7

Brown/Black

Structural meaning: 'Self-Disparagement'
Since this is a very negative meaning, this group is generally rejected and appears most often at the very end of the Eight-colour sequence. When it does appear at the beginning, it indicates the renunciation of everything except physical gratification because of a feeling of purposelessness.

7 0

Black/Grey

Structural meaning: 'Separative Isolation'
or   'Total Non-Involvement'
Considers the situation repugnant and wants nothing to do with it. Tries to shield himself from anything which might influence him.

71
Black/Blue

Structural meaning: 'Absolute Peace'
In revolt against the overall situation and just wants to be left in peace. Where this group appears towards one end of the row with 3 4 (or 4 3) towards the other, instability of the self-regulating nervous system should be suspected.

72
Black/Green

Structural meaning: 'Obstinate Exclusion'
or   'Prejudiced Self-Righteousness'
Revolt (7) followed by self-insistence (2) implies defiant obstinacy and rigid adherence to his own point of view.

73
Black/Red

Structural meaning: 'Exaggerated Desire'
or   'Dramatization'
Action based on and reinforced by revolt leads to impetuosity and extreme behaviour aimed at satisfying exaggerated desires.

74
Black/Yellow

Structural meaning: 'Sudden Crisis'
or   'Headstrong Decisions'
The two extremes of light and dark, with black revolt against fate followed by yellow hope of solving problems, leads to extreme actions and decisions, and the likelihood of resorting to desperate remedies.

75
Black/Violet

Structural meaning: 'Need for Identification'
or   'Compulsive Blending'
Insists (7) on identification (5). Things must fit together or blend perfectly, no concessions nor compromise being permissible.

76
Black/Brown

Structural meaning: 'Self-Disparagement'
As for 6 7, but with greater emphasis on revolt against events.

CHAPTER EIGHT

TEST INTERPRETATION

A Word of Warning

Nobody minds being told what a splendid fellow he is! On the other hand, many Eight-colour selections which may have to be interpreted suggest that things are far from being splendid, the test being heavily weighed down by anxieties, stress-sources and compensatory behaviour of a compulsive and often unwise nature. If an analysis of such a test is being given verbally, it is essential to pick one's words with great care so as to be helpful and constructive, rather than to be bluntly dogmatic, since the latter is not only likely to be wounding to the ego but can also be very destructive. If the report is to be written up for the individual concerned, one is not obliged to adhere to the actual wording of the Tables and it is usually better to put things into language which will communicate the ideas to the person concerned, while at the same time being careful to be as encouraging and constructive as possible.

The Eight-colour sequence, while demonstrably accurate enough in its analysis, nevertheless analyses and shows up an existing picture – it does not necessarily indicate whether this picture is the result of deep-seated psychogenic imbalance or whether it is the result of present or past environmental conditions affecting present behaviour. The Lüscher Eight-colour Test alone is not sufficient to allow this to be determined beyond question, and for this the Full Test (or some other 'deep test') must be resorted to.

Stress or environmental conditions which are intolerable and which lead to sub-optimum behaviour can and do affect the personality. However, this effect on the personality is not necessarily permanent; if found and recognized in time, steps can be taken to change the environment and provide more suitable conditions, in which the undesirable personality traits will begin to fall away. A test taken again after this has been done will show the improvement which has occurred, whether the improvement is one of personality or of health.

On the other hand, personality traits which have developed as a real or imagined defence against difficult environmental conditions will, if long continued, have a damaging effect on the deeper layers of the psyche. If this is allowed to happen, then a simple change of environment may no longer be enough and psychotherapeutic help of one sort or another may need to be resorted to.

It is therefore essential, when looking at a test in which all the wrong colours are in the wrong places and which has an allocation of twelve ! s, not to assume automatically that you should immediately send for a psychiatrist and a strait-jacket! It may well be the test of a psychologically healthy and normal individual who is finding existing conditions intolerable and reacting to them rather desperately. Examine the problems with him or, if it is your own test, examine your own problems. If you cannot see that the existing situation bears any relationship to the personality revealed by the test analysis, then find a psychologist who can administer a Full Lüscher Test, or some other 'deep' test, such as the Rorschach or the Minnesota Multiphasic Personality Inventory (MMPI).

The Full Lüscher Test shows far more than an individual's reactions to existing situations and his general effect-response behaviour; it shows also his habitual conditioned attitude, his unconscious attitudes in the fields of emotion, volition, action and aspiration, and the drives and needs buried deep in his psyche. Armed with this information, the psychologist, the psychiatrist, the psychoanalyst can not only arrive at a complete and accurate diagnosis but can also see more easily what is the best remedial action to take.

If, therefore, the interpretation which results from use of the Lüscher Eight-colour Test as described in this book causes any concern, the best advice is to follow the matter up to the next stage. Consult a physician or a psychologist and find out whether the situation is environmental, medical or due to psychogenic causes. Correct knowledge of a problem is far more than half the answer to it!

Examples of Test Analyses

Example 1: Executive Vice-president of large international firm.
54 years of age. Married.

!!	!!!	Total !s = 5	
C C	A	+ FUNCTION: +1 +0	
+ + × × = = − −		× FUNCTION: ×2 ×3	

1ST
SELECTION 1 0 2 3 5 6 7 4   = FUNCTION: = 6 = 5

2ND
SELECTION 1 0 2 3 6 5 7 4   − FUNCTION: − 7 − 4

+ + × × = = − − + − FUNCTION:
C C   A   +1 − 4,
                        +0 − 4
!!   !!!   Total !s = 5

EXISTING SITUATION (× FUNCTION): (× 2 × 3)

Authoritative, or in a position of authority but liable to feel that further progress is rendered problematical by existing difficulties. Perseveres despite opposition.

STRESS-SOURCES (– FUNCTION): (– 7 – 4)

Unfulfilled hopes have led to uncertainty and a tense watchfulness. Insists on freedom of action and resents any form of control other than that which is self-imposed. Unwilling to go without or to relinquish anything, demanding security as a protection against further setback or loss of position and prestige. Doubts that things will be any better in the future, this negative attitude leading him to exaggerate his claims and to refuse reasonable compromises.

RE-STRAINED CHARACTERISTICS (= FUNCTION): (= 6 = 5)

Egocentric and therefore quick to take offence. Able to obtain physical satisfaction from sexual activity but tends to hold aloof emotionally.

DESIRED OBJECTIVE (+ FUNCTION): (+ 1 + 0)

Needs release from stress. Longs for peace, tranquillity and contentment.

ACTUAL PROBLEMS (+ − FUNCTIONS): (+ 1 − 4)

1. Disappointment at the non-fulfilment of his hopes and the fear that formulating fresh goals will only lead to further setbacks have resulted in considerable anxiety. He is trying to escape from this into a peaceful and harmonious state or relationship which will protect him from dissatisfaction and lack of appreciation.

(+ 0 − 4)

2. If his proposed solution (above) fails to work, he withdraws and protects himself by an attitude of cautious reserve. Is liable to become moody and depressed.

SUMMARY: A man in an authoritative position who is persevering despite difficulties, but who no longer finds much pleasure in his lot. Has had setbacks and disappointments, now wanting nothing more than to be able to relax in peace and take things more easily. Gets little satisfaction from what he does, being cautious, reserved and pessimistic.

ADDITIONAL INFORMATION

A study of the text of this book will reveal certain additional details which can be included in a full analysis. Some examples of the type of information are set out below:

1. The close similarity between first and second selections (virtually identical) suggests a certain rigidity of outlook and a degree of emotional inflexibility (page 34).
2. His job (described here by the × function, × 2 × 3) follows immediately after the 'switching-off' grey,

indicating that he does it mechanically, without it really being a part of himself (pages 57–58).

3. His need for calm, orderliness of environment, freedom from upsets (1 in 1st position) is compensatory and therefore likely to be inappropriate as a method of handling his circumstances at times – for instance, by being too placid or over-tolerant in dealing with situations which might require firm handling (see pages 39–40 – compensations).

4. Rejected yellow (4 in 8th position) leads to discouragement, irritability and mistrust of the motives of others (page 70).

5. Tends to cling to the familiar (page 70 – rejected yellow and preferred blue) and therefore hangs on to his possessions and to the traditional way of doing things. He would be unwilling to gamble or take risks of any sort.

6. Unlikely to be very happy in his married life, which would be a rather masochistic type of attachment to which he would cling despite joylessness, rather than risk the unfamiliar (page 70).

7. Though the 'work-group' is not intact, yet the 2 and 3 are together in the × group, the 4 being rejected to 8th place. This implies that he tackles his work purposefully, wanting to enhance his prestige by doing it well, but that it gives him little pleasure (pages 52–55). He would be reluctant to effect changes or accept new ideas (rejected yellow).

8. If his business or domestic life were to become disturbed or erratic, his health might suffer (blue compensation as a need to recuperate – page 61).

9. From Chapter Seven (page 77 ff.): he wants 'an interval of tranquillity', his existing situation is one of 'purposeful activity', he feels any surrender to 'sensuousness' is inappropriate and he firmly rejects 'headstrong decisions' and dislikes 'crises'. From this, he would appear as a quiet, methodical man and a hard worker, but un-

imaginative, preferring things to follow traditional and well-beaten paths – by no means a 'ruthless tycoon'.

10. With five !s in both virtually identical selections, his attitude does not change readily. Only 18.2% of 'normal adults' would have a greater number of !s (Appendix 'A').

Example 2: Senior business executive.
48 years of age. Divorced.

	!		Total !s = 1
	C C C	A	+ FUNCTION: + 3
	+ + + × = = – –		= FUNCTION: × 2 × 4
1ST **SELECTION**	4 2 0 3 1 5 7 6		= FUNCTION: = 0 = 6, = 5 = 1
2ND **SELECTION**	3 2 4 0 .6 5 1 7		– FUNCTION: – 1, – 7
	+ × × = = = =		+ – FUNCTION: + 3 – 7, + 3 – 1
		– –	
	C	A A ·	
	!!	Total !s = 2	

EXISTING SITUATION (× FUNCTION): (× 2 × 4) He is trying to improve his position and prestige. Is dissatisfied with his existing circumstances and considers some improvement essential to his self-esteem.

97

STRESS-SOURCES (— FUNCTION): (— 7)

1. Intensely anxious to be independent, unhampered and free from any limitation or restriction other than those he imposes on himself by his own choice and decision. He feels he is not sufficiently in control of his own destiny.

2. Holding depletion and depression at bay by keeping active; refuses to let himself relax.

(— 1)

An existing situation or relationship is unsatisfactory, but he feels unable to change it to bring about the sense of belonging which he needs. He is unwilling to expose his vulnerability and therefore continues to resist this state of affairs, but feels dependent on the attachment. This not only depresses him but makes him irritable and impatient, producing considerable restlessness and the urge to get away from the situation, either actually or, at least, mentally. His ability to concentrate may suffer. Restless and dissatisfied.

RESTRAINED CHARACTERISTICS (= FUNCTION): (= 0 = 6) (= 5 = 1)

1. Willing to become emotionally involved and able to achieve satisfaction from sexual activity.

2. Feels rather isolated and alone, but is too reserved to allow himself to form deep attachments. Egocentric and therefore quick to take offence.

DESIRED OBJECTIVE (+ FUNC- TION): (+ 3)	Activity is directed towards success and conquest. Takes a delight in action, is intense, vital and animated, with the desire to live life to the full.

ACTUAL PROBLEMS (+ — FUNC- TIONS): **(+ 3 — 1)**	1. Fighting against restriction or limitation and insists on developing freely as a result of his own efforts. (+ 3 − 7) 2. Anxiety and a restless dissatisfaction, either with circumstances or with unfulfilled emotional demands, have produced stress. He tries to escape by intense activity, directed either towards personal success or a variety of experience.

SUMMARY: A capable and active man, who devotes himself rather compulsively to his work in his attempt to compensate for emotional nonfulfilment. Ambitious but restless, and likely to try his hand at many things. Becomes discontented when he finds conditions restrictive.

ADDITIONAL INFORMATION

1. The fact that he directs his energies into work of some sort is further supported by the coming together of the 'work-group' under even the slight pressure of concentrating on doing the test. This indicates that activity is his protection (pages 52–55).
2. The changes between first and second selections indicate flexibility of outlook (page 34).

3. The 'work-group' is intact, and right at the beginning, showing the ability to work long and continuously at a job he likes doing (page 53).

4. The initial 3 being compensatory, he is likely to immerse himself too deeply, or too compulsively, in his activities; for instance, becoming totally absorbed and failing to do something else which is more essential (pages 39–40 – compensations).

5. Rejected blue (1 in 7th position) leads to restlessness and a tendency to become dissatisfied. With black as an anxiety (7 in 8th position), this dissatisfaction is most likely to manifest itself where restrictive conditions prevail.

6. Grey (0) in the first half of the test indicates a 'switching-off'. Here it occurs after the full 'work-group', implying that he is only able to experience directly through his work and his activities (pages 58–59).

7. The + 3 − 1 'actual problem' suggests either a 'Don Juan syndrome' with its attendant sexual pursuit as an attempt to compensate for emotional non-fulfilment (he has been divorced), or a pursuit of vigorous and adventurous activity (page 62).

8. The integrity of the 'work-group' at the very beginning of the row indicates an absence of exhaustibility, suggesting reasonably good health and an alert, active body (page 53). This is supported by brown (6) in the 'indifferent' area (page 74).

9. While the first selection has only one ! and the second has two, nevertheless there is little to choose between them, the first selection having three Cs and one A, while the second has one C and two As. Two !s is about the average for 'normal adults' (Appendix 'A'), there being only 38% (based on a sample of 1,000 testees) who are better off so far as allocation of !s is concerned.

INTERPRETATION TABLES

IMPORTANT

The Lüscher Colour Test, despite the remarkable ease
and speed with which it can be administered, is a 'deep'
psychological test, developed for the use of psychiatrists, psychologists, physicians and those who are
professionally involved with the conscious and unconscious characteristics and motivations of others. It is
NOT a parlour game, and most emphatically it is not a
weapon to be used in a general contest of 'one-upmanship'.
It is therefore essential, when interpreting the test for
another individual, to preserve the professional nature
of the test, to give your interpretation in private to the
person directly concerned and to disclose nothing to any
other person.
Written reports, such as those on pages 93 and following, are sometimes useful – provided the language is
chosen with care to be helpful rather than destructive –
but, in general, a verbal interpretation is best because
the various points raised can be discussed as they come
up. In this way it is usually possible to persuade the
person to see that what you are telling him is correct,
even though there may have been some initial resistance;
to do this increases his insight and his ability to deal
with or handle his problems. Responsible use of the
interpretations in the following Tables will invariably
prove useful and constructive.
Psychiatrists and analysts have to deal mainly with
neurosis, psychosis or emotional maladjustment, and
in such cases the interpretations derived from the Colour
Test have a particular significance. Where there is no
particular neurosis, and we are dealing with a 'normal'
situation, then the interpretation must be adapted to this
more normal state of affairs.

INTERPRETATION TABLES

Table I: The + Functions: *Desired Objectives*, or Behaviour Dictated by Desired Objectives.

Table II: The × Functions: *The Existing Situation*, or Behaviour Appropriate to the Existing Situation.

Table III: The = Functions: *Characteristics under Restraint*, or Behaviour Inappropriate to the Existing Situation.

Table IV: The — Functions: *Rejected or Suppressed Characteristics*, or Anxiety-Laden Characteristics.

Table V: The + — Functions: *The 'Actual Problem'*, or Behaviour Resulting from Stress.

Colour selections which are psychologically less desirable are indicated in the Tables by the assignment of one, two or three asterisks (*). The greater the number of asterisks, the further removed from the norm is that particular colour or group of colours.

Appendix 'B' (page 190) contains a table showing all possible groups and single colours, together with the relevant assignments of none, one, two or three *s.

TABLE I: + FUNCTIONS

A percentage figure is shown next to all + and all — combinations in the Eight-colour tables, eg, the figure of 0.6% appears next to the + 0 + 1 combination. These percentages state the average frequency of selection of each colour combination and were derived from the results of 36,892 tests administered to male students ranging in age from twenty to thirty years.

+ 0 . . . . Grey/. . . .

+ 0

Grey
2.7%

Unwilling to participate and wishes to avoid all forms of stimulation. Has had to put up with too much of a tiring or exhausting nature and now desires protection and non-involvement.

*

+ 0 + 1

Grey/Blue
0.6%

Feels exhausted by conflict and quarrelling and desires protection from them. Needs peaceful conditions and a tranquil environment in which to relax and recover.

*

+ 0 + 2

Grey/Green
0.4%

Feels the existing circumstances are hostile and is exhausted by conflict and quarrelling. Wishes to protect himself and hides his intentions to avoid exposing them to attack, so that they will be safer and easier to achieve. Careful to avoid stirring up any opposition which might endanger his plans.

*

+ 0 + 3

Grey/Red
0.5%

Has exaggerated demands on life which are concealed behind specious rationalization and cautious behaviour. Wishes to impress others with his achievements, but camouflages this desire and is inclined to be covert.

*

+ 0 + 4

Grey/Yellow
0.3%

Desires release from an unsatisfactory situation and from existing burdens which are both depressing and intolerable. Seeking a way out, but feels there is no solution. Tries to protect himself against becoming involved in arguments and conflict.

**

+ 0 + 5

Grey/Violet
0.2%

Fascinated by the idea of an idealized association of tenderness and mutual enchantment. Embarrassed by the thought of allowing this to appear openly, and so employs cautious exploratory tactics in the pursuit of this objective, making sure that he is neither irrevocably committed nor found out.

*

+ 0 + 6

Grey/Brown
0.6%

Desires protection against anything which might exhaust or tire him. Seeks a life of security and physical ease, free from any problem or disturbance.

**

+ 0 + 7

Grey/Black
0.2%

Feels he has been unjustly and undeservedly treated and betrayed in his hopes. Disgruntled and in revolt against his existing circumstances which he considers an affront.

***

+ 1

Blue
15.9%

Desires a tranquil, peaceful state of harmony offering quiet contentment and a sense of belonging.

+ 1 + 0

Blue/Grey
1.2%

Needs release from stress. Longs for peace, tranquillity and contentment.

+ 1 + 2

Blue/Green
3.8%

Needs a peaceful environment. Wants release from stress, and freedom from conflicts or disagreement. Takes pains to control the situation and its problems by proceeding cautiously. Has sensitivity of feeling and a fine eye for detail.

+ 1 + 3

Blue/Red
3.6%

Seeks affectionate, satisfying and harmonious relationships. Desires an intimate union, in which there is love, self-sacrifice and mutual trust.

+ 1 + 4

Blue/Yellow
1.4%

Seeks an affectionate relationship, offering fulfilment and happiness. Capable of powerful emotional enthusiasm. Helpful, and willing to adapt himself if necessary to realize the bond of affection he desires. Needs the same consideration and understanding from others.

+ 1 + 5

Blue/Violet
4.4%

Longs for tenderness and for a sensitivity of feeling into which he can blend. Responsive to anything aesthetic and tasteful.

+ 1 + 6

Blue/Brown
.1%

Desires a conflict-free haven offering security and physical ease. Is in need of considerate treatment and loving care. Fears the emptiness and solitude of separation.

*

+ 1 + 7

Blue/Black
.5%

Urgently in need of rest, relaxation, peace and affectionate understanding. Feels he has been treated with a lack of consideration and is upset and agitated as a result. Regards his situation as intolerable as long as his requirements are not complied with.

**

+2....Green/....

+ 2

Green
18.1%

Seeks the determination and elasticity of will necessary to establish himself and to make himself independent despite the difficulties of his situation. Wants to overcome opposition and achieve recognition.

+ 2 + 0

Green/Grey
0.7%

Wants to establish himself and make an impact despite unfavourable circumstances and a general lack of appreciation.

*

+ 2 + 1

Green/Blue
3.5%

Wants to make a favourable impression and be recognized. Needs to feel appreciated and admired. Sensitive and easily hurt if no notice is taken of him or if he is not given adequate acknowledgement.

+ 2 + 3

Green/Red
5.2%

Seeks success. Wants to overcome obstacles and opposition and to make his own decisions. Pursues his objectives single-mindedly and with initiative. Does not want to feel dependent on the goodwill of others.

+2+4

Green/Yellow
2.3%

Needs recognition. Ambitious, wants to impress and be looked up to, to be both popular and admired. Seeks to bridge the gap which he feels separates him from others.

+2+5

Green/Violet
4.2%

Wants to make a favourable impression and be regarded as a special personality. Is therefore constantly on the watch to see whether he is succeeding in this and how others are reacting to him; this makes him feel that he is in control. Uses tactics cleverly in order to obtain influence and special recognition. Susceptible to the aesthetic or original.

+2+6

Green/Brown
1.8%

Feels too much is being asked of him and is tired out, but still wants to overcome his difficulties and establish himself despite the effect such an effort would have on him. Proud, but resigned in his attitude. Needs recognition, security and fewer problems.

*

+2+7

Green/Black
0.5%

Wants to prove to himself and others that nothing can affect him, that he is superior to any form of weakness. As a result, he acts with harshness or severity and adopts an autocratic and self-willed attitude.

**

+3.... Red/....

+3

Red
28.9%

Intense, vital and animated, taking a delight in action. Activity is directed towards success or conquest and there is a desire to live life to the full.

+ 3 + 0

Red/Grey
9.9%

Wants to sweep aside the things that stand in his way, to follow his impulses and be involved in special or exciting happenings. In this way he hopes to deaden the intensity of his conflicts, but his impulsive behaviour leads him to take risks.

*

+ 3 + 1

Red/Blue
4.4%

Strives for a life rich in activity and experience, and for a close bond offering sexual and emotional fulfilment.

+ 3 + 2

Red/Green
6.6%

Pursues his objectives with intensity and does not allow himself to be deflected from his purpose. Wants to overcome the obstacles with which he is faced and to achieve special recognition and standing from his success.

+ 3 + 4

Red/Yellow
11.0%

Seeks success, stimulation and a life full of experience. Wants to develop freely and to shake off the shackles of self-doubt, to win and to live intensely. Likes contacts with others and is enthusiastic by nature. Receptive to anything new, modern or intriguing; has many interests and wants to expand his fields of activity. Optimistic about the future.

+ 3 + 5

Red/Violet
3.5%

Preoccupied with things of an intensely exciting nature, whether erotically stimulating or otherwise. Wants to be regarded as an exciting and interesting personality with an altogether charming and impressive influence on others. Uses tactics skilfully so as to avoid endangering his chances of success or undermining others' confidence in himself.

+ 3 + 6

Red/Brown
2.1%

Shelves his ambitions and forgoes his desire for prestige as he prefers to take things easily and indulge his longing for comfort and security.   ★

+ 3 + 7

Red/Black
0.3%

Wants to make up for what he feels he has missed by living with exaggerated intensity; in this way he feels he can break free from all the things that oppress him.   ★★

+ 4 .... Yellow/....

+ 4

Yellow
12.5%

Needs a change in his circumstances or in his relationships which will permit relief from stress. Seeking a solution which will open up new and better possibilities and allow hopes to be fulfilled.   ★

+ 4 + 0

Yellow/Grey
0.5%

Needs a way of escape from all that oppresses him and is clinging to vague and illusory hopes.   ★★

+ 4 + 1

Yellow/Blue
1.2%

Hopes that ties of affection and good-fellowship will bring release and contentment. His own need for approval makes him ready to be of help to others and in exchange he wants warmth and understanding. Open to new ideas and possibilities which he hopes will prove fruitful and interesting.   ★

+ 4 + 2

Yellow/Green
2.2%

Alert and keenly observant. Is seeking fresh avenues offering greater freedom and the chance to make the most of them. Wants to prove himself and to achieve recognition. Striving to bridge the gap which he feels separates him from others.   ★

+ 4 + 3

Yellow/Red
6.7%

His need to feel more causative and to have a wider sphere of influence makes him restless and he is driven by his desires and hopes. May try to spread his activities over too wide a field.

*

+ 4 + 5

Yellow/Violet
1.2%

Over-imaginative and given to fantasy or day-dreaming. Longs for interesting and exciting things to happen and wants to be admired for his charm.

*

+ 4 + 6

Yellow/Brown
0.6%

In despair and needs relief of some sort. Wants physical ease, a problem-free security and the chance to recover.

**

+ 4 + 7

Yellow/Black
0.3%

Tries to escape from his problems, difficulties and tensions by abrupt, head-strong and ill-considered decisions or changes of direction.

***

+ 5 . . . . Violet/. . . .

+ 5

Violet
15.3%

Needs to feel identified with someone or something and wishes to win support by his charm and amiability. Sentimental, and yearns for a romantic tenderness.

+ 5 + 0

Violet/Grey
0.3%

Longs for sensitive and sympathetic understanding and wants to protect himself against argument, conflict or any exhausting stresses.

*

+ 5 + 1

Violet/Blue
4.1%

Longs for a tender and sympathetic bond and for a situation of idealized harmony. Has an imperative need for tenderness and affection. Susceptible to anything aesthetic.

+5 +2
Violet/Green
4.8%

Wants to make a favourable impression and be regarded as a special personality. Is therefore constantly on the watch to see whether he is succeeding in this and how others are reacting to him; this makes him feel that he is in control. Uses tactics cleverly in order to obtain influence and special recognition. Susceptible to the aesthetic or original.

+5 +3
Violet/Red
3.3%

Takes easily and quickly to anything which provides stimulation. Preoccupied with things of an intensely exciting nature, whether erotically stimulating or otherwise. Wants to be regarded as an exciting and interesting personality with an altogether charming and impressive influence on others. Uses tactics cleverly so as to avoid endangering his chances of success or undermining others' confidence in himself.

+5 +4
Violet/Yellow
1.8%

Wants interesting and exciting things to happen. Able to make himself well-liked by his obvious interest and by the very openness of his charm. Over-imaginative and given to fantasy or day-dreaming.

+5 +6
Violet/Brown
0.6%

Wishes to find his stimulation in a voluptuous atmosphere of sensuous luxury.

+5 +7
Violet/Black
0.4%

Has an imperative need for some bond or fusion with another which will prove sensually fulfilling, but which will not conflict with his convictions or sense of fitness.

+6.... Brown/....

+6

Brown

.7%

Seeks freedom from problems and a secure state of physical ease in which to relax and recover.

*

+6+0

Brown/Grey

.6%

Badly in need of rest and relaxation, freedom from conflict and the chance to recover. Wants to protect himself against destructive and exhausting influences. Longs for security and freedom from problems.

**

+6+1

Brown/Blue

.7%

Wants contentment, physical ease and the absence of conflict. Needs security and clings to it so as not to have to suffer loneliness or separation.

*

+6+2

Brown/Green

.2%

Keeps himself under strict control so as not to break down under his difficulties. Needs a safer and easier situation in which he can feel more secure and have a chance to recover.

*

+6+3

Brown/Red

.1%

Has a powerful drive towards sensuousness.

*

+6+4

Brown/Yellow

.5%

Feels that there is little prospect of achieving his hopes and therefore surrenders himself to a life of sensuous ease, free from any problems.

**

113

+6+5

Brown/Violet
0.4%

Seeks luxury, sensuous comfort and the indulgence of a taste for the voluptuous.

+6+7

Brown/Black
0.2%

Sets himself idealistic but illusory goals. Has been bitterly disappointed and turns his back on life in a weary self-disgust. Wants to forget it all and recover in a comfortable, problem-free situation. ★★

+7.... Black/....

+7

Black
1.8%

Considers the existing circumstances disagreeable and over-demanding. Refuses to allow anything to influence his point of view. ★★

+7+0

Black/Grey
0.3%

Feels the situation is hopeless. Strongly resists those things which he finds disagreeable (see the interpretations for − 1, − 2, − 3 or − 4, whichever of these is appropriate). Tries to shield himself from anything which might irritate him or make him feel more depressed. ★★★

+7+1

Black/Blue
0.4%

Suffering from the effects of those things which are being rejected as disagreeable (see the interpretations for − 2, − 3 or − 4, whichever of these is appropriate), and is strongly resisting them. Just wants to be left in peace. ★

+7+2

Black/Green
0.3%

Defiantly opposes any sort of restriction or opposition. Sticks obstinately to his own point of view in the belief that this proves his independence and self-determination. ★

+ 7 + 3

Black/Red
0.2%

Suffering from pent-up over-stimulation which threatens to discharge itself in an outburst of impulsive and impassioned behaviour.   **

+ 7 + 4

Black/Yellow
0.3%

Tries to escape from his problems, difficulties and tensions by abrupt, headstrong and ill-considered decisions. Desperately seeking a way of escape, and there is danger of reckless behaviour to the point of self-destruction.   ***

+ 7 + 5

Black/Violet
0.2%

Demands that ideas and emotions shall merge and blend perfectly. Refuses to make any concessions or to accept any compromises.   **

+ 7 + 6

Black/Brown
0.1%

Sets himself idealistic but illusory goals. Has been bitterly disappointed and turns his back on life in weary self-disgust. Wants to forget it all and recover in a comfortable, problem-free situation.   ***

TABLE II: ✕ FUNCTIONS

✕ 0 . . . Grey/. . .

✕ 0

Grey

This represents a barrier between the compensatory colours which precede it and the remaining colours – the point at which 'switching-off' has occurred. The + group is thus the sole mechanism through which participating experience is possible. Emphasizes the characteristics of the + group and makes them more compulsive.

✕ 0 ✕ 1

Grey/Blue

Relatively inactive and in a static condition, while conflict of one sort or another prevents peace of mind. Unable to achieve relationships of the desired degree of mutual affection and understanding. (The + group is an attempt to compensate for this and other conflicts.)

✕ 0 ✕ 2

Grey/Green

The situation is difficult and he is trying to persist in his objectives against resistance. Finds it necessary to conceal his intentions as an added precaution, in order to disarm opposition. (The + group is an attempt to compensate for this and other conflicts.)

✕ 0 ✕ 3

Grey/Red

Having difficulty in making progress. Despite the attempt to conceal impulsiveness, his activities lead to problems and uncertainties, making him tense and irritable. (The + group is an attempt to compensate for this and other conflicts.)

× 0 × 4

Grey/Yellow

Non-realization of hopes and the inability to decide on necessary remedial action has resulted in considerable stress. (The + group is an attempt to compensate for this and other conflicts.)

× 0 × 5

Grey/Violet

The fear of rebuff and the extreme caution of his approach make it difficult for him to achieve the degree of intimacy and identification he desires.

× 0 × 6

Grey/Brown

Unable to exert the effort to achieve his objectives. Feels neglected, desiring greater security, warm affection and fewer problems. (The + group is an attempt to compensate for this and other conflicts.)

× 0 × 7

Grey/Black

Under considerable stress due to the demands of the existing situation. Trying to extricate himself from the things which restrict him or tie him down. (The + group is an attempt to compensate for this and other conflicts.)

*

+ 1 . . . . Blue/. . . .

× 1

Blue

Acts calmly, with the minimum of upset, in order to handle existing relationships. Likes to feel relaxed and at ease with his associates and those close to him.

× 1 × 0

Blue/Grey

Sensitive and understanding but under some strain; needs to unwind in the company of someone close to him.

✕ 1 ✕ 2

Blue/Green

Acts in an orderly, methodical and self-contained manner. Needs the sympathetic understanding of someone who will give him recognition and approval.

✕ 1 ✕ 3

Blue/Red

Works well in cooperation with others but is disinclined to take the leading role. Needs a personal life of mutual understanding and freedom from discord.

✕ 1 ✕ 4

Blue/Yellow

Willing and adaptable. Only at peace when closely attached to a person, group or organization on which reliance can be placed.

✕ 1 ✕ 5

Blue/Violet

Sensitive; needs aesthetic surroundings, or an equally sensitive and understanding partner with whom to share a warm intimacy.

✕ 1 ✕ 6

Blue/Brown

Avoids excessive effort and needs roots, security and peaceful companionship.

✕ 1 ✕ 7

Blue/Black

Needs warm companionship, but is intolerant of anything short of special consideration from those close to him. If this is not forthcoming, is liable to shut himself away from them.

✕ 2 . . . . Green/. . . .

✕ 2

Green

Persistent. Demands what he feels to be his due and endeavours to maintain his position intact.

× 2 × 0
Green/Grey

Defensive. Feels his position is threatened or inadequately established. Determined to pursue his objectives despite the anxiety induced by opposition.

× 2 × 1
Green/Blue

Orderly, methodical and self-contained. Needs the respect, recognition and understanding of those close to him.

× 2 × 3
Green/Red

Authoritative or in a position of authority, but liable to feel that further progress is rendered problematical by existing difficulties. Perseveres despite opposition.

× 2 × 4
Green/Yellow

Trying to improve his position and prestige. Dissatisfied with his existing circumstances and considers some improvement essential to his self-esteem.

× 2 × 5
Green/Violet

Working to improve his image in the eyes of others in order to obtain their compliance and agreement with his needs and wishes.

× 2 × 6
Green/Brown

Working to create for himself a firm foundation on which to erect a secure, comfortable and problem-free future, in which he will be granted respect and recognition.

× 2 × 7
Green/Black

Pursues his objectives and his own self-interest with stubborn determination; refuses to compromise or make concessions.

× 3 . . . . Red/. . . .

× 3

Red

Active, but feels that insufficient progress is being made or insufficient reward being obtained for the effort exerted.

× 3 × 0

Red/Grey

Impulsive and irritable. His desires, and the actions involved, are paramount, insufficient consideration being given to their consequences. This leads to, or arises from, stress and conflict.

× 3 × 1

Red/Blue

Works well in cooperation with others. Needs a personal life of mutual understanding and freedom from discord.

× 3 × 2

Red/Green

Exercises initiative in overcoming obstacles and difficulties. Either holds, or wishes to achieve, a position of authority in which control can be exerted over events.

× 3 × 4

Red/Yellow

Volatile and outgoing. Needs to feel that events are developing along desired lines, otherwise irritation can lead to changeability or superficial activities.

× 3 × 5

Red/Violet

Readily participates in things affording excitement or stimulation. Wants to feel exhilarated.

× 3 × 6

Red/Brown

Unwilling to extend himself or exert undue effort (with the possible exception of sexual activity). Feels that further progress requires more from him than he is willing or able to give. Would prefer reasonable comfort and security rather than the rewards of a greater ambition.

✗ 3 ✗ 7

Red/Black

Feels obstructed in his desires and prevented from obtaining the things he regards as essential. (The + group is an attempt to compensate for this and other conflicts.)

    *

✗ 4 . . . . Yellow/. . . .

✗ 4

Yellow

Attracted by anything new, modern or intriguing. Liable to be bored by the humdrum, the ordinary or the traditional.

✗ 4 ✗ 0

Yellow/Grey

Is seeking a solution to existing problems or anxieties, but is liable to find it difficult to decide on a right course to follow.

✗ 4 ✗ 1

Yellow/Blue

Easily affected by his environment and readily moved by the emotions of others. Seeks congenial relationships and an occupation which will promote them.

✗ 4 ✗ 2

Yellow/Green

Hopes to obtain an improved position and greater prestige, so that he can procure for himself more of the things he has had to do without.

✗ 4 ✗ 3

Yellow/Red

Active, outgoing and restless. Feels frustrated by the slowness with which events develop along the desired lines. This leads to irritability, changeability and lack of persistence when pursuing a given objective.

✗ 4 ✗ 5

Yellow/Violet

Imaginative and sensitive; seeking an outlet for these qualities – especially in the company of someone equally sensitive. Interest and enthusiasm are readily aroused by the unusual or the adventurous.

× 4 × 6

Yellow/Brown

Insecure. Seeks roots, stability, emotional security and an environment providing greater ease and fewer problems.

× 4 × 7

Yellow/Black

The existing situation contains critical or dangerous elements for which it is imperative that some solution be found. This may lead to sudden, even reckless, decisions. Self-willed and rejects any advice from others. (The + group is an attempt to compensate for this and other conflicts.)

*

× 5 . . . . Violet/. . . .

× 5

Violet

Seeks to express the need for identification in a sensitive and intimate atmosphere where aesthetic or emotional delicacy can be protected and nurtured.

× 5 × 0

Violet/Grey

Seeks a close and understanding bond in an atmosphere of shared intimacy, as a protection against anxiety and conflict.

× 5 × 1

Violet/Blue

Seeks to share a bond of understanding intimacy in an aesthetic atmosphere of peace and tenderness.

× 5 × 2

Violet/Green

Working to improve his image in the eyes of others so as to obtain their compliance and agreement with his needs and wishes.

× 5 × 3

Violet/Red

Readily participates in things affording excitement or stimulation. Wants to feel exhilarated.

× 5 × 4

Violet/Yellow

Imaginative and sensitive; seeking an outlet for these qualities – especially in the company of someone equally sensitive. Interest and enthusiasm are readily aroused by the unusual or the adventurous.

× functions

× 6 . . . .
brown/

× 5 × 6

Violet/Brown

Sensuous. Inclined to luxuriate in things which give gratification to the senses, but rejects anything tasteless, vulgar or coarse.

× 5 × 7

Violet/Black

Needs, and insists on having, a close and understanding relationship, or at least some method of satisfying a compulsion to feel identified.

× 6 . . . . Brown/. . . .

× 6

Brown

Uneasy and insecure in the existing situation. Needs greater security and a more affectionate environment, or a situation imposing less physical strain. (The + group is an attempt to compensate for this and other conflicts.)

*

× 6 × 0

Brown/Grey

Unable to exert the effort to achieve his objectives. Feels neglected, desiring greater security, warm affection and fewer problems. (The + group is an attempt to compensate for this and other conflicts.)

*

× 6 × 1

Brown/Blue

Avoids excessive effort and needs roots, security and peaceful companionship. May be physically unwell, in need of gentle handling and considerate treatment.

× 6 × 2

Brown/Green

Having difficulty in standing up to the demands imposed on him. Finds a great effort is involved and wishes to have the situation eased.

× 6 × 3

Brown/Red

Having difficulty in making progress and unwilling to put forth further effort. Seeking more comfortable conditions where he can avoid anything disturbing.

× 6 × 4

Brown/Yellow

Insecure. Seeks roots, stability, emotional security and an environment providing greater ease and fewer problems, but is either unwilling or unable to exert the effort.

× 6 × 5

Brown/Violet

Sensuous. Inclined to luxuriate in things which give gratification to the senses, but rejects anything tasteless, vulgar or coarse.

× 6 × 7

Brown/Black

Physical illness, over-tension or emotional distress have taken a severe toll. His self-esteem has been reduced and he now needs peaceful conditions and considerate treatment to permit recovery. (The + group is an attempt to compensate for this and other conflicts.)   *

× 7 Black). . . .

× 7

Black

Conflict and dissatisfaction of one sort or another enforce the need for the compensations indicated by the + group.   *

× 7 × 0

Black/Grey

Dissatisfied. The need to escape continued involvement with his present circumstances makes it imperative for him to find some solution. (The + group indicates the compensatory method likely to be adopted.)   **

× 7 × 1
Black/Blue

Needs peace and quiet. Desires a close and faithful partner from whom to demand special consideration and unquestioning affection. If these requirements are not met, is liable to turn away and withdraw altogether. (The requirements he demands from his environment or from the partner will be indicated in the + group.)   *

× 7 × 2
Black/Green

Not only considers his demands minimal, but also regards them as imperative. Sticks to them stubbornly and will concede nothing. (The + group is an attempt to compensate for this and other conflicts.)   *

× 7 × 3
Black/Red

Feels obstructed in his desires and prevented from obtaining the things he regards as essential. (The + group is an attempt to compensate for this and other conflicts.)   *

× 7 × 4
Black/Yellow

The existing situation contains critical or dangerous elements for which it is imperative that some solution be found. This may lead to sudden, even reckless, decisions. Self-willed and rejects any advice from others. (The + group is an attempt to compensate for this and other conflicts.)   *

× 7 × 5
Black/Violet

Needs, and insists on having, a close and understanding relationship, or at least some method of satisfying a compulsion to feel identified. (The + group is an attempt to compensate for this and other conflicts.)   *

× 7 × 6

Black/Brown

Physical illness, over-tension or emotional distress have taken a severe toll. His self-esteem has been reduced and he now needs peaceful conditions and considerate treatment to permit recovery. (The **+** group is an attempt to compensate for this and other conflicts.)　　**✷✷**

TABLE III: = FUNCTIONS

= 0 . . . . Grey/. . . .

= 0

Grey

Willing to participate and to allow himself to become involved, but tries to fend off conflict and disturbance in order to reduce tension.

= 0 = 1

Grey/Blue

Relationships rarely measure up to his high emotional expectations and his need to be made much of, leading to disappointment (often characteristic of mother-fixation, taking the form of either strong attachment to, or resentment of, the mother). Always has mental reservations and tends to remain emotionally isolated and unattached.

= 0 = 2

Grey/Green

Feels he is receiving less than his share, but that he will have to conform and make the best of his situation.

= 0 = 3

Grey/Red

Feels listless, hemmed in and anxious; considers that circumstances are forcing him to restrain his desires. Wants to avoid open conflict with others and to have peace and quiet.   *

= 0 = 4

Grey/Yellow

Demanding and particular in his relations with his partner or those close to him, but careful to avoid open conflict since this might reduce his prospects of realizing his hopes and ideas.

= 0 = 5

Grey/Violet

Egocentric and therefore quick to take offence.

127

= 0 = 6

Grey/Brown

Willing to become emotionally involved and able to achieve satisfaction from sexual activity.

= 0 = 7

Grey/Black

Circumstances are such that he feels forced to compromise for the time being if he is to avoid being cut off from affection or from full participation.

= 1 .... Blue/....

= 1

Blue

Remains emotionally unattached even when involved in a close relationship.

= 1 = 0

Blue/Grey

Has high emotional demands and is willing to involve himself in a close relationship, but not with any great depth of feeling.

= 1 = 2

Blue/Green

Believes that he is not receiving his share – that he is neither properly understood nor adequately appreciated. Feels that he is being compelled to conform, and close relationships leave him without any sense of emotional involvement.

= 1 = 3

Blue/Red

Feels cut off and unhappy because of the difficulty in achieving the essential degree of cooperation and harmony which he desires.

*

= 1 = 4

Blue/Yellow

Exacting in his emotional demands and very particular in his choice of partner. The desire for emotional independence prevents any depth of involvement.

= 1 = 5
Blue/Violet

Egocentric and therefore quick to take offence, leaving him rather isolated in his attachments.

= 1 = 6
Blue/Brown

Able to obtain physical satisfaction from sexual activity but is inclined to be emotionally withdrawn, which prevents him from becoming deeply involved.

= 1 = 7
Blue/Black

Emotionally inhibited. Feels forced to compromise, making it difficult for him to form a stable emotional attachment.

= 2 . . . . Green/. . . .

= 2
Green

The situation is preventing him from establishing himself, but he feels he must make the best of things as they are.

= 2 = 0
Green/Grey

An unadmitted lack of confidence makes him careful to avoid open conflict and he feels he must make the best of things as they are.

= 2 = 1
Green/Blue

Believes that he is not receiving his share – that he is neither properly understood nor adequately appreciated. Feels that he is being compelled to conform, and close relationships leave him without any sense of emotional involvement.

= 2 = 3
Green/Red

Unhappy at the resistance he feels whenever he tries to assert himself. Indignant and resentful because of these setbacks, but gives way apathetically and makes whatever adjustments are necessary so that he can have peace and quiet.

*

129

= 2 = 4

Green/Yellow

Feels that he is burdened with more than his fair share of problems. However, he sticks to his goals and tries to overcome his difficulties by being flexible and accommodating.

= 2 = 5

Green/Violet

Feels that he is receiving less than his share and that there is no one on whom he can rely for sympathy and understanding. Pent-up emotions make him quick to take offence, but he realizes that he has to make the best of things as they are.

= 2 = 6

Green/Brown

Feels that he cannot do much about his existing problems and difficulties and that he must make the best of things as they are. Able to achieve satisfaction through sexual activity.

= 2 = 7

Green/Black

Circumstances are forcing him to compromise, to restrain his demands and hopes, and to forgo for the time being some of the things he wants.

= 3 . . . . Red/. . . .

= 3

Red

Trying to calm down and unwind after a period of over-agitation which has left him listless and devoid of energy. In need of peace and quiet; becomes irritable if this is denied him.

*

= 3 = 0

Red/Grey

Distressed by the obstacles with which he is faced and in no mood for any form of activity or for further demands on him. Needs peace and quiet, and the avoidance of anything which might distress him further.

*

= 3 = 1

Red/Blue

Feels cut off and unhappy because of the difficulty in achieving the essential degree of cooperation and harmony which he desires.

*

= 3 = 2

Red/Green

Unhappy at the resistance he feels whenever he tries to assert himself. However, he believes that there is little he can do and that he must make the best of the situation.

*

= 3 = 4

Red/Yellow

Wants to broaden his fields of activity and insists that his hopes and ideas are realistic. Distressed by the fear that he may be prevented from doing what he wants; needs both peaceful conditions and quiet reassurance to restore his confidence.

*

= 3 = 5

Red/Violet

Becomes distressed when his needs or desires are misunderstood and feels that he has no one to turn to or rely on. Egocentric and therefore quick to take offence.

*

= 3 = 6

Red/Brown

Feels trapped in a distressing or uncomfortable situation and seeking some way of gaining relief. Able to achieve satisfaction from sexual activity.

*

= 3 = 7

Red/Black

Circumstances are restrictive and hampering, forcing him to forgo all joys and pleasures for the time being.

*

= 4 . . . . Yellow/. . . .

= 4

Yellow

Clings to his belief that his hopes and ideals are realistic, but needs encouragement and reassurance. Applies very exacting standards to his choice of a partner and wants guarantees against loss or disappointment.

= 4 = 0

Yellow/Grey

Willing to become emotionally involved, but demanding and particular in his choice of a partner and in his relations with those close to him. Needs reassurance and is careful to avoid open conflict since this might reduce his prospects of realizing his hopes.

= 4 = 1

Yellow/Blue

Exacting in his emotional demands, especially during moments of intimacy, leaving him frustrated in his desire for a perfect union.

= 4 = 2

Yellow/Green

Feels that he is burdened with more than his fair share of problems. However, he sticks to his goals and tries to overcome his difficulties by being flexible and accommodating.

= 4 = 3

Yellow/Red

Wants to broaden his fields of activity and insists that his hopes and ideas are realistic. Distressed by the fear that he may be prevented from doing what he wants; needs both peaceful conditions and quiet reassurance to restore his confidence.

*

= 4 = 5

Yellow/Violet

Insists that his hopes and ideas are realistic, but needs reassurance and encouragement. Egocentric and therefore quick to take offence.

= 4 = 6

Yellow/Brown

Very exacting in the standards he applies to his choice of a partner and seeking a rather unrealistic perfection in his sex life.

= 4 = 7

Yellow/Black

Insists that his goals are realistic and sticks obstinately to them, even though circumstances are forcing him to compromise. Very exacting in the standards he applies to his choice of a partner.

= 5 . . . . Violet/. . . .

= 5

Violet

Egocentric and therefore quick to take offence. Sensitive and sentimental, but conceals this from all except those very close to him.

= 5 = 0

Violet/Grey

Willing to become emotionally involved as he feels rather isolated and alone. Egocentric and therefore quick to take offence, though he tries to avoid open conflict.

= 5 = 1

Violet/Blue

Feels rather isolated and alone, but is too reserved to allow himself to form deep attachments. Egocentric and therefore quick to take offence.

= 5 = 2

Violet/Green

Feels that he is receiving less than his share and that there is no one on whom he can rely for sympathy and understanding. Pent-up emotions and a certain egocentricity make him quick to take offence, but he realizes that he has to make the best of things as they are.

= 5 = 3

Violet/Red

Becomes distressed when his needs or desires are misunderstood and feels that he has no one to turn to or rely on. Egocentric and therefore quick to take offence.

*

= 5 = 4

Violet/Yellow

Insists that his hopes and ideas are realistic, but needs reassurance and encouragement. Egocentric and therefore quick to take offence.

= 5 = 6

Violet/Brown

Egocentric and therefore quick to take offence. Able to obtain physical satisfaction from sexual activity but tends to hold aloof emotionally.

= 5 = 7

Violet/Black

Conditions are such that he will not let himself become intimately involved without making mental reservations.

= 6 . . . . Brown/. . . .

= 6

Brown

Able to achieve satisfaction from sexual activity.

= 6 = 0

Brown/Grey

Willing to become emotionally involved and able to achieve satisfaction through sexual activity, but tries to avoid conflict.

= 6 = 1

Brown/Blue

Able to achieve physical satisfaction from sexual activity but restless and inclined to be emotionally withdrawn, which prevents him from becoming deeply involved.

= 6 = 2

Brown/Green

Feels that he cannot do much about his existing problems and difficulties and that he must make the best of things as they are. Able to achieve physical satisfaction from sexual activity.

= 6 = 3

Brown/Red

Feels trapped in a distressing or uncomfortable situation and seeking some way of gaining relief. Able to achieve satisfaction through sexual activity providing no turmoil or emotional agitation is involved.

*

= 6 = 4

Brown/Yellow

Very exacting in the standards he applies to his choice of a partner and seeking a rather unrealistic perfection in his sex life.

= 6 = 5

Brown/Violet

Egocentric and therefore quick to take offence. Able to obtain physical satisfaction from sexual activity but tends to hold aloof emotionally.

= 6 = 7

Brown/Black

Circumstances force him to compromise and to forgo some pleasures for the time being. Capable of achieving physical satisfaction from sexual activity.

= 7 . . . . Black/. . .

= 7

Black

Feels that things stand in his way, that circumstances are forcing him to compromise and forgo some pleasures for the time being.

= 7 = 0

Black/Grey

Circumstances are such that he feels forced to compromise for the time being if he is to avoid being cut off from affection or from full participation.

= 7 = 1

Black/Blue

Emotionally inhibited. Feels forced to compromise, making it difficult for him to form a stable emotional attachment.

= 7 = 2

Black/Green

Circumstances are forcing him to compromise, to restrain his demands and hopes, and to forgo for the time being some of the things he wants.

= 7 = 3

Black/Red

Circumstances are restrictive and hampering, forcing him to forgo all joys and pleasures for the time being.

*

= 7 = 4

Black/Yellow

Insists that his goals are realistic and sticks obstinately to them, even though circumstances are forcing him to compromise. Very exacting in the standards he applies to his choice of a partner.

= 7 = 5

Black/Violet

Conditions are such that he will not let himself become intimately involved without making mental reservations.

136

= functions

= 7 = 6
Black/Brown

Circumstances force him to compromise and to forgo some pleasures for the time being. Capable of achieving physical satisfaction through sexual activity.

TABLE IV: — FUNCTIONS

A percentage figure is shown next to all + and all — combinations in the Eight-colour tables, eg, the figure of 0.9% appears next to the — 0 — 1 combinations. These percentages state the average frequency of selection of each colour combination and were derived from the results of 36,892 tests administered to male students ranging in age from twenty to thirty years.

— 0 . . . . Grey/. . . .

— 0

Grey
21.1%

Physiological interpretation: displays impatience and agitation (in 8th position, and especially when classed as an 'anxiety').

Psychological interpretation: feels that life has far more to offer and that there are still important things to be achieved – that life must be experienced to the full. As a result, he pursues his objectives with a fierce intensity and will not let go of things. Becomes deeply involved and runs the risk of being unable to view things with sufficient objectivity, or calmly enough; is therefore in danger of becoming agitated and of exhausting his nervous energy. Cannot leave things alone and feels he can only be at peace when he has finally reached his goal.

In brief: impatient involvement.

— 0 — 1

Grey/Blue
0.9%

Physiological interpretation: refuses to relax or give in. Holding exhaustion and depression at bay by keeping active (especially in 7th & 8th positions; but also, to a lesser extent, in 6th & 7th).

Psychological interpretation: an existing situation or relationship is unsatisfactory, but he feels unable to change it to bring about the sense of belonging which he needs. Unwilling to expose his vulnerability, therefore continues to resist this state of affairs, but feels dependent on the attachment. This not only depresses him but makes him irritable and impatient, producing considerable restlessness and the urge to get away from the situation, either actually or, at least, mentally. Ability to concentrate may suffer.

In brief: restless dissatisfaction.   **

(The **+** group is therefore needed as a compensation.)

— 0 — 2
Grey/Green
0.4%

Physiological interpretation: will power and perseverance are in danger of being overwhelmed by excessive stress (especially in 7th & 8th positions, but also in 6th & 7th).

Psychological interpretation: resilience and tenacity have become weakened. Feels overtaxed, worn out and getting nowhere, but continues to stand his ground. He feels this adverse situation as an actual tangible pressure which is intolerable to him and from which he wants to escape, but he feels unable to make the necessary decision.

In brief: unresolved pressure.   **

(The **+** group is therefore needed as a compensation.)

— 0 — 3
Grey/Red
0.5%

Physiological interpretation: suppressed agitation resulting from the attempt to resist any form of stimulation or excitement. Can lead to irritability, angry outbursts or even sexual neuroses. There is a possibility of cardiac complaints.

Psychological interpretation: the situation is regarded as threatening and dangerous. Outraged at the thought that he will be unable to achieve his goals and distressed at his feeling of helplessness to remedy this. Over-extended and feels beset, possibly to the point of nervous prostration.
In brief: helpless irritability.   **
(The + group is therefore needed as a compensation.)

— 0 — 4
Grey/Yellow
1.7%

Physiological interpretation: stresses resulting from disappointment have led to agitation (especially in 7th & 8th positions, but also, to a lesser extent, in 6th & 7th).
Psychological interpretation: unfulfilled expectations have led to uncertainty and an apprehensive watchfulness. Badly needs to feel secure and protected against further disappointment, being passed over, or losing standing and prestige. Doubtful that things will be any better in the future, but inclined nevertheless to make exaggerated demands and to reject compromise.
In brief: apprehensive insecurity.   **
(The + group is therefore needed as a compensation.)

— 0 — 5
Grey/Violet
1.7%

Physiological interpretation: stress due to suppressed sensitivity (in 7th & 8th positions, and especially when classed as an 'anxiety').
Psychological interpretation: Delights in the tasteful, the gracious and the sensitive, but maintains his attitude of critical appraisal and refuses to be swept off his feet unless genuineness and integrity can be absolutely vouched for. Therefore keeps a

strict and watchful control on his emotional relationships as he must know
exactly where he stands. Demands complete sincerity as a protection against his
own tendency to be too trusting.
In brief: controlled responsiveness.

— 0 — 6

Grey/Brown
3.8%

Physiological interpretation: suppression
of the physical and nervous requirements
of the body (in 7th & 8th positions, and
especially when classed as an 'anxiety').
Psychological interpretation: the existing
situation is disagreeable. Has an unsatisfied need to ally himself with others whose
standards are as high as his own, and to
stand out from the rank and file. His control of his sensual instincts restricts his
ability to give himself, but the resulting
isolation leads to the urge to surrender
and allow himself to merge with another.
This disturbs him, as such instincts are
regarded as weaknesses to be overcome;
he feels that only by continued self-
restraint can he hope to maintain his
attitude of individual superiority. Wants to
be loved or admired for himself alone;
needs attention, recognition and the
esteem of others.
In brief: demands esteem as an exceptional individual.

— 0 — 7

Grey/Black
15.3%

Physiological interpretation: pronounced
susceptibility to outside stimuli (in 7th &
8th positions, and especially when classed
as an 'anxiety').
Psychological interpretation: wants to overcome a feeling of emptiness and to bridge
the gap which he feels separates him from
others. Anxious to experience life in all its

141

aspects, to explore all its possibilities and to live it to the full. He therefore resents any restriction or limitation being imposed on him and insists on being free and unhampered.
In brief: expectant self-determinism.

– 1 . . . . Blue/. . . .

– 1

Blue
4.7%

Physiological interpretation: refuses to relax or give in. Holding exhaustion and depression at bay by keeping active (especially in 8th position; far less so in 6th position).
Psychological interpretation: an existing situation or relationship is unsatisfactory, but he feels unable to change it to bring about the sense of belonging which he needs. Unwilling to expose his vulnerability, he therefore continues to resist this state of affairs, but feels dependent on the attachment. This not only depresses him, but makes him irritable and impatient, producing considerable restlessness and the urge to get away from the situation, either actually or, at least, mentally. Ability to concentrate may suffer.
In brief: restless dissatisfaction.   *
(The + group is therefore needed as a compensation.)

– 1 – 0

Blue/Grey
1.5%

Physiological Interpretation: displays impatience and restlessness and inclined to be depressed (in 7th & 8th positions).
Psychological interpretation: feels he cannot control the situation to create the sense of belonging he needs, and so re-

mains unwilling to place himself unreservedly in another's hands. Is resisting a condition or a relationship which he regards as a discouraging responsibility. Feels life has far more to offer and is likely to remain impatient and irritable until he has obtained all he feels he still lacks. The urge to get away from this unsatisfactory state leads to restlessness and instability. Concentration may suffer.

In brief: restless and impatient non-fulfilment.   *

(The + group is therefore needed as a compensation.)

−1−2

Blue/Green
0.2%

Physiological interpretation: will power and perseverance are in danger of being overwhelmed by excessive stress. (Especially in 7th & 8th positions, but also in 6th & 7th).

Psychological interpretation: resilience and tenacity are being overtaxed by the continued attempt to overcome existing difficulties. Sticks to his objectives but feels subjected to intolerable pressure. Considers it impossible to change the situation into one of cooperation and mutual trust and so desires to be free of it altogether.

In brief: pressure arising from stress and discord.   ***

(The + group is therefore needed as a compensation.)

−1−3

Blue/Red
0.2%

Physiological interpretation: suppressed agitation resulting from unsatisfactory or discordant personal relationships. Can lead to irritability, angry outbursts or sexual neuroses. There is a possibility of cardiac complaints.

Psychological interpretation: considerable distress is arising from some unsatisfactory relationship. He feels helpless to restore affinity and any semblance of mutual trust, so the situation is regarded as a depressing and unhappy state which he must continue to tolerate. Beset to the point of nervous prostration.

In brief: helpless and irritable disharmony. ***
(The + group is therefore needed as a compensation.)

— 1 — 4

Blue/Yellow
0.3%

Physiological interpretation: stress and anxiety have resulted from emotional disappointment (especially in 7th & 8th positions, but also in 6th & 7th).

Psychological interpretation: an emotional relationship is no longer running smoothly, has proved deeply disappointing and is now regarded as a depressing tie. While on the one hand, he would like to free himself from this attachment altogether, yet, on the other, he does not want to lose anything nor risk uncertainty and the possibility of further disappointment. These contradictory emotions aggravate him to such an extent that he tries to suppress them beneath an aloof and severe attitude.

In brief: stress arising from emotional disappointment. ***
(The + group is therefore needed as a compensation.)

— 1 — 5

Physiological interpretation: stress arising from lack of mutual understanding (es-

**Blue/Violet
2.0%**

pecially in 7th & 8th positions; less so in 6th & 7th).

Psychological interpretation: an existing situation is unsatisfactory and he feels unable to improve it without willing cooperation. The need for understanding and for affectionate give-and-take remains unsatisfied; he now has a feeling of being tied down, giving rise to impatience, irritability and the desire to escape.

In brief: impatience arising from continued misunderstanding.

(The **+** group is therefore needed as a compensation.)

                                           *

**−1 − 6

Blue/Brown
0.6%**

Physiological interpretation: emotional discontent and lack of appreciation have led to stress and excessive self-restraint (in 7th & 8th positions; far less significant in 6th & 7th positions).

Psychological interpretation: feels he must have cooperation before the existing situation can be improved. Lack of understanding and appreciation makes him feel no real bond exists, and discontent gives rise to a touchy sensitivity; he wants to feel safer and more at ease. He would like to get away from what he now considers a depressing tie and re-establish his own Individuality. His sensual self-restraint makes it difficult for him to give himself, but the resulting isolation leads to the urge to surrender and merge with another. This disturbs him as he regards such instincts as weaknesses to be overcome – he feels that he can only assert his own individuality by continued self-restraint,

that this alone will allow him to stand his
ground through his present difficulties.
In brief: emotional discontent arising
from lack of appreciation and undue self-
restraint.   *

(The + group is therefore needed as a
compensation.)

— 1 — 7

Blue/Black
4.9%

Physiological interpretation: emotional
dissatisfaction has given rise to a touchy
and impatient desire for independence,
leading to stress and restlessness (in 7th
& 8th positions; less severe in 6th & 7th).
Psychological interpretation: an existing
situation or relationship is unsatisfactory,
but he feels unable to improve it without
willing cooperation. Unwilling to expose
his vulnerability and therefore considers
it inadvisable to display affection or be
over-demonstrative. He regards the relationship as a depressing tie but, although
he wants to be independent and unhampered, he does not want to risk losing anything. All this leads him to react touchily
and with impatience, while the urge to
'get away from it all' results in considerable restlessness. The ability to concentrate may suffer.
In brief: restless instability arising from
emotional dissatisfaction.   *

(The + group is therefore needed as a
compensation.)

— 2 . . . . Green/ . . . .

— 2

Green
2.8%

Physiological interpretation: will power,
resilience and the ability to stand up to
opposition are in danger of being overwhelmed by excessive stress (especially

146

in 8th position; in 6th position this is less pronounced, but still present.)

Psychological interpretation: the tenacity and strength of will necessary to contend with existing difficulties has become weakened. Feels overtaxed, worn out and getting nowhere. but continues to stand his ground. He feels this adverse situation as an actual tangible pressure which is intolerable to him and from which he wants to escape, but he feels unable to make the necessary decision.

In brief: reluctance to take the steps necessary to resolve a stress situation. **

(The **+** group is therefore needed as a compensation.)

− 2 − 0
Green/Grey
0.7%

Physiological interpretation: the ability to withstand pressure has been overtaxed, leading to stress and frustration, impatience and irritability (especially in 7th & 8th positions; but also, to a lesser extent, in 6th & 7th).

Psychological interpretation: has lost the resilience and strength of will necessary to contend with existing difficulties. Feels overtaxed and getting nowhere, but continues to stand his ground and still pursues his objectives with a fierce intensity. This subjects him to intolerable pressure from which he wants to escape, but he cannot bring himself to make the necessary decision. As a result he remains firmly involved in the problem and can neither view it objectively nor get rid of it − he cannot leave it alone and feels he will only be at peace when he has reached his objective.

In brief: unresolved involvement. **

(The **+** group is therefore needed as a compensation.)

— 2 — 1

Green/Blue
0.3%

Physiological interpretation: emotional dissatisfaction and reduced ability to withstand opposition or difficulties are producing stress and frustration.

Psychological interpretation: has lost the resilience and strength of will necessary to contend with existing difficulties, which appear to him as deliberate opposition. Stands his ground, but is subjected to intolerable pressure. Needs cooperation and emotional fulfilment and feels that, in their absence, there is nothing he can do to improve the current situation. Wants to 'get away from it all' quickly.

In brief: pressure arising from stress and discord. **

(The + group is therefore needed as a compensation.)

— 2 — 3

Green/Red
0.2%

Physiological interpretation: distress and agitation resulting from the attempt to avoid any form of stimulation or excitement. Regards his environment as hostile and is under great pressure. Irritable or angry outbursts, with the possibility of sexual neuroses or cardiac complaints.

Psychological interpretation: distressed by the apparent hostility of the environment. Feels coerced and subjected to intolerable pressure. Is rebellious and resentful of what he regards as unreasonable demands on him, but feels powerless to control the situation and unable to protect himself.

In brief: helpless rebelliousness. **

(The + group is therefore needed as a compensation.)

— 2 — 4

Green/Yellow
0.4%

Physiological interpretation: stress and anxiety due to conflict between hope and necessity, following acute disappointment.
Psychological interpretation: disappointment and unfulfilled hopes have given rise to an anxious uncertainty, while doubts that things will be any better in the future lead to the postponement of essential decisions. This conflict between hope and necessity is creating considerable pressure. Instead of resolving this by facing up to making the essential decision, he is likely to immerse himself in the persuit of trivialities as an escape route.
In brief: frustrated vacillation.   ***
(The + group is therefore needed as a compensation.)

— 2 — 5

Green/Violet
1.0%

Physiological interpretation: stress resulting from a feeling of belittlement and misunderstanding (especially in 7th & 8th positions; materially less in 6th & 7th positions.)
Psychological interpretation: feels in an invidious position: that trust, affection and understanding are being withheld and that he is being treated with a humiliating lack of consideration. Considers he is being denied the appreciation essential to his self-esteem and that there is nothing he can do about it. Disheartened by the lone struggle against difficulties with no encouragement. Feels he is getting nowhere; that, instead of the admiration he needs, he is consistently misunderstood. Wants to escape from the situation but cannot find the strength of mind to make the necessary decision.
In brief: humiliated by lack of appreciation.
(The + group is therefore needed as a compensation.)

— 2 — 6

Green/Brown
0.7%

Physiological interpretation: stress resulting from excessive self-restraint in the attempt to win the regard and esteem of others (especially in 7th & 8th positions; materially less in 6th & 7th positions).

Psychological interpretation: has an unsatisfied need to ally himself with others whose standards are as high as his own, and to stand out from the rank and file. This subjects him to considerable stress, but he sticks to his attitudes despite lack of appreciation. Finds the situation uncomfortable and would like to break away from it, but refuses to compromise with his opinions. Unable to resolve the situation because he continually postpones making the necessary decision as he doubts his ability to withstand the opposition which would result. Needs the esteem of others, compliance with his wishes and respect for his opinions before he can feel at ease and secure.

In brief: stubborn but ineffectual demand for esteem.   ⋆

(The + group is therefore needed as a compensation.)

— 2 — 7

Green/Black
1.7%

Physiological interpretation: frustration at unacceptable restrictions on his freedom of action is producing stress (especially in 7th & 8th positions; materially less in 6th & 7th positions).

Psychological interpretation: seeks independence and freedom from any restriction and therefore avoids obligations or anything which might prove hampering. He is being subjected to considerable pressure and wants to escape from it so that he can obtain what he needs, but tends to lack the necessary strength of purpose to succeed in this.

In brief: frustrated desire for independence and freedom of action.

(The + group is therefore needed as a compensation.)

*

— 3 . . . . Red/. . . .

— 3

Red
3.4%

Physiological interpretation: suppressed and pent-up agitation resulting from the attempt to resist any additional stimulation, leading to irritability, angry outbursts or even sexual neuroses. There is a possibility of cardiac trouble. (Especially significant in 8th position, but still present in 6th position.)

Psychological interpretation: the situation is regarded as threatening and dangerous. Outraged by the thought that he will be unable to achieve his goals and distressed at the feeling of helplessness to remedy this. Over-extended and feels beset, possibly to the point of nervous prostration.

In brief: helplessness.

**

(The + group is therefore needed as a compensation.)

— 3 — 0

Red/Grey
0.8%

Physiological interpretation: suppressed agitation resulting from the attempt to resist any additional stimulation. Impatient, erratic and irritable, with the possibility of hypertension or other cardiac trouble. (Especially in 7th & 8th positions, but also, to a lesser extent, in 6th & 7th positions.)

Psychological interpretation: the situation is regarded as threatening and dangerous: Resentful that what he has striven so hard

for is being menaced, and desperate because he feels powerless to prevent
it – fears that he is going to miss out altogether. Unable to view the situation objectively, but extremely agitated and cannot
rest in his attempts to remove this threat
to his desires. Over-extended and feels
beset, possibly to the point of nervous
prostration.
In brief: desperate agitation.   **
(The **+** group is therefore needed as a
compensation.)

— 3 — 1

Red/Blue
0.2%

Physiological interpretation: suppressed
agitation resulting from the attempt to
resist any additional stimulation combined with the inability to relax cause him
to drive himself beyond the capacity of
his resources. Impatient, irritable and hectic, with the possibility of hypertension or
other cardiac trouble.
Psychological interpretation: distressed by
the unsatisfactory state of some close
association. Feels unable to do anything
to restore affinity and mutual trust, and
considers that he is tied down in an unhappy situation from which he cannot
escape.
In brief: distress resulting from disharmony.   ***
(The **+** group is therefore needed as a
compensation.)

— 3 — 2

Red/Green
0.1%

Physiological interpretation: agitated helplessness and inability to control events
are subjecting him to great stress. Possibility of cardiac trouble and/or muscular
spasm.

Psychological interpretation: acutely distressed by what appears as a hostile environment. Feels he is being subjected to intolerable pressure and driven against his will. Rebellious and resentful at what he considers unreasonable demands on him, but feels powerless to control the situation or protect himself in any way.
In brief: helpless resentment.   ***
(The **+** group is therefore needed as a compensation.)

— 3 — 4
Red/Yellow
1.5%

Physiological interpretation: stresses resulting from disappointment have led to agitation and anxiety.
Psychological interpretation: eager to make a good impression, but worried and doubtful about the likelihood of succeeding. Feels that he has a right to anything he might hope for, and becomes helpless and distressed when circumstances go against him. Finds the mere possibility of failure most upsetting and this can even lead to nervous prostration. Sees himself as a 'victim' who has been misled and abused, mistakes this dramatization for reality and tries to convince himself that his failure to achieve standing and recognition is the fault of others.
In brief: unrealistic self-justification.   ***
(The **+** group is therefore needed as a compensation.)

— 3 — 5
Red/Violet
0.8%

Physiological interpretation: stress resulting from frustration in his attempts to achieve security and understanding (especially in 7th & 8th positions: materially less in 6th & 7th positions).
Psychological interpretation: is responsive

to outside stimuli and wants to experience everything intensely, but is finding the existing situation extremely frustrating. Needs sympathetic understanding and a sense of security. Distressed by his apparent powerlessness to achieve his goals.

In brief: frustrated empathy.   **

(The + group is therefore needed as a compensation.)

— 3 — 6

Red/Brown
0.7%

Physiological interpretation: tension arising from nervous prostration or from sexual stress, due to excessive self-restraint. (In 7th & 8th positions; minor in 6th & 7th).

Psychological interpretation: feels unappreciated and finds the existing situation disagreeable. Wants personal recognition and the esteem of others to compensate for the lack of like-minded people with whom to ally himself and make himself more secure. His sensual self-restraint makes it difficult for him to give himself, but the resulting isolation leads to the urge to surrender and merge with another. This disturbs him as he regards such instincts as weaknesses to be overcome; only by not succumbing to them, he feels, can he withstand the difficulties of the situation. Wants to be valued as a desirable associate and admired for his personal qualities.

In brief: insecurity arising from lack of allies.   *

(The + group is therefore needed as a compensation.)

— 3 — 7

Red/Black
0.9%

Physiological interpretation: stress arising from the frustrations of an unwanted situation (mainly in 7th & 8th positions; less so in 6th & 7th).

Psychological interpretation: feels trapped in a disagreeable situation and powerless to remedy it. Angry and disgruntled as he doubts that he will be able to achieve his goals and frustrated almost to the point of nervous prostration. Wants to get away, feel less restricted and free to make his own decisions.

In brief: frustrated desire for independence.   *

(The **+** group is therefore needed as a compensation.)

— 4 . . . . Yellow/. . . .

— 4

Yellow
8.6%

Physiological interpretation: stresses resulting from disappointment have led to agitation (especially in 8th position; far less so in 6th position).

Psychological interpretation: unfulfilled hopes have led to uncertainty and apprehension. Needs to feel secure and to avoid any further disappointment, and fears being passed over or losing standing and prestige. Doubts that things will be any better in the future and this negative attitude leads him to make exaggerated demands and to refuse to make reasonable compromises.

In brief: agitated pessimism; fearful of losing prestige.   **

(The **+** group is therefore needed as a compensation.)

− 4 − 0

Yellow/Grey
2.1%

Physiological interpretation: uncertainty and worry over missing opportunities have have led to a condition of agitated tension (especially in 7th & 8th positions; materially less in 6th & 7th positions).

Psychological interpretation: feels that life must yield more than it is and that his hopes and desires must somehow be realized – that they must be granted in their entirety. The existing uncertainty causes considerable worry and he is tensely on his guard against missing any opportunity. Anxious to avoid further setbacks, any loss of standing or prestige. Tries to make sure that he will not be overlooked and badly needs security.

In brief: tensely expectant.

(The **+** group is therefore needed as a compensation.)

    *

− 4 − 1

Yellow/Blue
0.2%

Physiological interpretation: stress and anxiety have resulted from emotional disappointment (especially in 7th & 8th positions, but also in 6th & 7th).

Psychological interpretation: an emotional relationship is no longer running smoothly, has proven deeply disappointing and is now regarded as a depressing tie. While on the one hand, he would like to free himself from this attachment altogether, yet, on the other, he does not want to lose anything nor risk uncertainty and the possibility of further disappointment. These contradictory emotions aggravate him to such an extent that he tries to suppress them beneath an aloof and severe attitude.

In brief: stress arising from emotional disappointment.

(The **+** group is therefore needed as a compensation.)

    ***

— 4 — 2
Yellow/Green
0.2%

Physiological interpretation: stress and anxiety due to conflict between hope and necessity, following acute disappointment.

Psychological interpretation: disappointment and unfulfilled hopes have given rise to an anxious uncertainty, while doubts that things will be any better in the future lead to the postponement of essential decisions. This conflict between hope and necessity is creating considerable pressure. Instead of resolving this by facing up to making the essential decision, he is likely to immerse himself in the pursuit of trivialities as an escape route.

In brief: frustrated vacillation.   ***

(The + group is therefore needed as a compensation.)

— 4 — 3
Yellow/Red
0.9%

Physiological interpretation: stresses resulting from disappointment have led to agitation and anxiety.

Psychological interpretation: eager to make a good impression, but worried and doubtful about the likelihood of succeeding. Feels that he has a right to anything he might hope for, and becomes helpless and distressed when circumstances go against him. Finds the mere possibility of failure most upsetting and this can even lead to nervous prostration. Sees himself as a 'victim' who has been misled and abused, mistakes this dramatization for reality, and tries to convince himself that his failure to achieve standing and recognition is the fault of others.

In brief: unrealistic self-justification.   ***

(The + group is therefore needed as a compensation.)

— 4 — 5

Yellow/Violet
1.2%

Physiological interpretation: disappointment had led to a suspicious, restrained withdrawal from others and into himself (in 7th & 8th positions; far less in 6th & 7th.)

Psychological interpretation: suppresses his innate enthusiasm and imaginative nature, for fear that he might be carried away by it only to find himself pursuing some will-o'-the-wisp. Feels he has been misled and abused and has withdrawn to hold himself cautiously aloof from others. Keeps a careful and critical watch to see whether motives towards him are sincere – a watchfulness which easily develops into suspicion and distrust.

In brief: 'Once bitten, twice shy'; emotional disappointment leading to watchful mistrust of motive. *

(The + group is therefore needed as a compensation.)

— 4 — 6

Yellow/Brown
1.1%

Physiological interpretation: stress resulting from the effort to conceal worry and anxiety under a cloak of self-reliance and unconcern (mainly in 7th & 8th positions; far less in 6th & 7th).

Psychological interpretation: the existing situation is disagreeable. Feels lonely and uncertain as he has an unsatisfied need to ally himself with others whose standards are as high as his own, and wants to stand out from the rank and file. This sense of isolation magnifies the need into a compelling urge, all the more upsetting to his self-sufficiency because of the restraint he normally imposes on himself. Since he wants to demonstrate the unique quality of his own character, he tries to suppress this need for others and affects an attitude of unconcerned self-reliance to conceal his fear of inadequacy, treating those who criticize his behaviour with contempt. However, beneath this assumption of indifference he really longs for the approval and esteem of others.

In brief: disappointment leading to assumed indifference. *

(The + group is therefore needed as a compensation.)

— 4 — 7

Yellow/Black
3.4%

Physiological interpretation: stress resulting from disappointment and watchful self-protection against further setback (mainly in 7th & 8th positions).

Psychological interpretation: unfulfilled hopes have led to uncertainty and a tense watchfulness. Insists on freedom of action and resents any form of control other than that which is self-imposed. Unwilling to go without or to relinquish anything and demands security as a protection against any further setback or loss of position and prestige. Doubts that things will be any better in the future and this negative attitude leads him to exaggerate his claims and to refuse reasonable compromises.

In brief: watchful and retentive. *

(The + group is therefore needed as a compensation.)

— 5 . . . . Violet/. . . .

— 5

Violet
11.0%

Physiological interpretation: stress due to suppressed sensitivity (in 8th position only; mild if not classed as an 'anxiety').

Psychological interpretation: delights in

the tasteful, the gracious and the sensitive, but maintains his attitude of critical appraisal and refuses to be swept off his feet unless genuiness and integrity can be absolutely vouched for. Therefore keeps a strict and watchful control on his emotional relationships as he must know exactly where he stands. Demands complete sincerity as a protection against his own tendency to be too trusting.
In brief: controlled and analytical responsiveness.

— 5 — 0

Violet/Grey
1.7%

Physiological interpretation: displays impatience and agitation (in 7th & 8th positions only; mild if not classed as an 'anxiety').
Psychological interpretation: feels that life has far more to offer and that it is imperative that he should find the responsive and understanding relationship he is seeking; he therefore follows up any opportunity which presents itself. However, he maintains his attitude of critical appraisal and refuses to be swept off his feet unless genuineness and integrity can be absolutely vouched for. Therefore keeps a strict and watchful control on his emotional relationships as he must know exactly where he stands. Demands complete sincerity as a protection against his own tendency to be too trusting.
In brief: controlled responsiveness.

— 5 — 1

Violet/Blue
0.9%

Physiological interpretation: refuses to relax or give in. Holding exhaustion and depression at bay by keeping active (especially in 7th & 8th positions; rather less in 6th & 7th).

Psychological interpretation: an existing relationship is unsatisfactory but he feels unable to change it without cooperation; the need for understanding, for affection-ate give-and-take remains unfulfilled. This not only depresses him but makes him irritable and impatient, producing restlessness and the urge to get away from the situation, either actually or, at least, mentally. Ability to concentrate may suffer.

In brief: restlessness due to emotional dissatisfaction.   *

(The **+** group is therefore needed as a compensation.)

— 5 — 2

Violet/Green
0.5%

Physiological interpretation: stress re-sulting from the feeling of belittlement and misunderstanding (especially in 7th & 8th positions; slightly less in 6th & 7th).

Psychological interpretation: feels in an invidious position, that trust, affection and understanding are being withheld and that he is being treated with an humiliating lack of consideration. Con-siders he is being denied the appreciation essential to his self-esteem and that there is nothing he can do about it. Disheartened by the lone struggle against difficulties with no encouragement. Feels he is get-ting nowhere; that, instead of the admira-tion he needs, he is consistently misunderstood. Wants to escape from the situation but cannot find the strength of mind to make the necessary decision.

In brief: humiliated by lack of appreciation.   *

(The **+** group is therefore needed as a compensation.)

— 5 — 3

Violet/Red
0.3%

Physiological interpretation: stress resulting from frustration in his attempts to achieve security and understanding. Nervous strength can become seriously depleted and there is a possibility of cardiac trouble (especially in 7th & 8th positions; slightly less in 6th & 7th).

Psychological interpretation: Is responsive to outside stimuli and wants to experience everything intensely, but is finding the existing situation extremely frustrating. Needs sympathetic understanding and a sense of security. Distressed by his apparent powerlessness to achieve his goals.

In brief: emotional and empathic frustration.   **★★**

(The **+** group is therefore needed as a compensation.)

— 5 — 4

Violet/Yellow
0.9%

Physiological interpretation: disappointment has led to a suspicious and restrained withdrawal from others and into himself (especially in 7th & 8th positions; less in 6th & 7th).

Psychological interpretation: suppresses his innate enthusiasm and imaginative nature, for fear he might be carried away by it only to find himself pursuing some will-o'-the-wisp. Feels he has been misled and abused and has withdrawn to hold himself cautiously aloof from others. Keeps a careful and critical watch to see whether motives towards him are sincere – a watchfulness which easily develops into suspicion and distrust.

In brief: 'Once bitten, twice shy'; emotional disappointment, leading to watchful mistrust of motive.   **★**

(The **+** group is therefore needed as a compensation.)

— 5 — 6
Violet/Brown
1.0%

Physiological interpretation: stress arising from the inability to maintain relationships stably in their desired condition (in 7th & 8th positions only; mild if not classed as an 'anxiety').

Psychological interpretation: wants a partner with whom he can share fully in an atmosphere of cloudless serenity, but his compulsion to demonstrate his individuality leads him to adopt a critical and demanding attitude. This introduces discord and leads to alternating periods of drawing closer and drawing apart, so that the ideal state he desires is not allowed to develop. Despite the urge to gratify his natural desires, he imposes a considerable self-restraint on his instincts in the belief that this demonstrates his superiority and raises him above the common herd. Discerning, critical and particular, having taste and discrimination. These qualities, combined with his tendency to form his own views, enable him to judge things for himself and to express his opinions with authority. He enjoys the original, the ingenious and the subtle, striving to ally himself with others of similar taste who can help him in his intellectual unfolding. Desires admiration and the esteem of others.

In brief: intellectual or aesthetic discrimination.

— 5 — 7
Violet/Black
3.6%

Physiological interpretation: stress resulting from unwelcome restriction or limitation (only if classed as an 'anxiety' in 7th & 8th positions).

Psychological interpretation: strives for straight-forward relationships, founded on mutual trust and understanding. Wishes to act only in conformity with his own convictions. Demands freedom to make his own decisions without being subjected to interference, outside influence or the necessity of making compromises.

In brief: demands independence and 'straight dealing'.

— 6 . . . . Brown/. . . .

— 6

Brown
11.4%

Physiological interpretation: stress arising from suppression of physical or sexual desires and insufficient consideration for bodily needs (in 8th position only and especially if classed as an 'anxiety').
Psychological interpretation: has an unsatisfied need to ally himself with others whose standards are as high as his own, and to stand out from the common herd. This desire for pre-eminence isolates him and inhibits his readiness to give himself freely. While he wants to surrender and let himself go, he regards this as a weakness which must be resisted. This self-restraint, he feels, will lift him above the rank and file and ensure recognition as a unique and distinctive personality.
In brief: demands esteem from others.

— 6 — 0

Brown/Grey
5.8%

Physiological interpretation: stress arising from suppression of physical or sexual desires and insufficient consideration for bodily needs (in 7th & 8th positions only and especially if classed as an 'anxiety').
Psychological interpretation: the existing

situation is disagreeable. Has an unsatisfied need to ally himself with others whose standards are as high as his own, and to stand out from the common herd. His control of his sensual instincts restricts his ability to give himself, but the resulting isolation leads to the urge to surrender and allow himself to merge with another. This disturbs him, as such instincts are regarded as weaknesses to be overcome; he feels that only by continued self-restraint can he hope to maintain his attitude of individual superiority. Wants to be loved or admired for himself alone; needs attention, recognition and the esteem of others.
In brief: demands esteem as an exceptional individual.

— 6 — 1

Brown/Blue
0.5%

Physiological interpretation: emotional discontent and lack of appreciation have led to stress and excessive self-restraint (in 7th & 8th positions; less pronounced in 6th & 7th positions).
Psychological interpretation: feels he must have cooperation before the existing situation can be improved. Lack of understanding and appreciation makes him feel no real bond exists, and discontent gives rise to a touchy sensitivity; he wants to feel safer and more at ease. He would like to get away from what he now considers a depressing tie and re-establish his own individuality. His sensual self-restraint makes it difficult for him to give himself, but the resulting isolation leads to the urge to surrender and merge with another. This disturbs him, as he regards such instincts as weaknesses to be overcome; he feels that he can only assert his own

individuality by continued self-restraint
and that this alone will allow him to stand
his ground through his present difficulties.
In brief: emotional discontent arising
from lack of appreciation and undue self-
restraint.   *

(The **+** group is therefore needed as a
compensation.)

– 6 – 2

Brown/Green
0.2%

Physiological interpretation: stress resulting from excessive self-restraint in the
attempt to win the regard and esteem of
others (especially in 7th & 8th positions;
less pronounced, but still significant, in
6th & 7th).

Psychological interpretation: has an unsatisfied need to ally himself with others
whose standards are as high as his own,
and to stand out from the rank and file.
This subjects him to considerable stress,
but he sticks to his attitudes despite lack
of appreciation. Finds the situation uncomfortable and would like to break away
from it, but refuses to compromise with
his opinions. Unable to resolve the situation because he continually postpones
making the necessary decision, as he
doubts his ability to withstand the opposition which would result. Needs the esteem
of others, compliance with his wishes
and respect for his opinions before he can
feel at ease and secure.

In brief: stubborn but ineffectual demand
for esteem.   *

(The **+** group is therefore needed as a
compensation.)

— 6 — 3
Brown/Red
0.6%

Physiological interpretation: stress arising from suppression of physical or sexual desires and insufficient consideration of bodily needs (especially in 7th & 8th positions; slightly less acute in 6th & 7th).

Psychological interpretation: feels unappreciated and finds the existing situation threatening. Wants personal recognition and the esteem of others to compensate for the lack of like-minded people with whom to ally himself and make himself more secure. His sensual self-restraint makes it difficult for him to give himself, but the resulting isolation leads to the urge to surrender and merge with another. This disturbs him, as he regards such instincts as weaknesses to be overcome; he feels that only in this way can he withstand the difficulties of the situation. Wants to be valued as a desirable associate and be admired for his personal qualities.

In brief: insecurity arising from lack of allies. **

(The + group is therefore needed as a compensation.)

— 6 — 4
Brown/Yellow
1.3%

Physiological interpretation: stress resulting from the effort to conceal worry and anxiety under a cloak of self-reliance and unconcern (especially in 7th & 8th positions; less pronounced, but still significant, in 6th & 7th).

Psychological interpretation: the existing situation is disagreeable. Feels lonely and uncertain as he has an unsatisfied need to ally himself with others whose standards are as high as his own and to stand out from the rank and file. This sense of isolation magnifies his need into a compelling urge, all the more upsetting to his self-sufficiency because of the restraint he normally imposes on himself. Since he wants to demonstrate the unique quality of his own character, he tries to suppress this need for others, and affects an attitude of unconcerned self-reliance to conceal his fear of inadequacy, treating those who criticize his behaviour with contempt. However, beneath this assumption of indifference he really longs for the approval and esteem of others.

In brief: disappointment leading to assumed indifference.

(The **+** group is therefore needed as a compensation.)

— 6 — 5

Brown/Violet
1.5%

Physiological interpretation: stress arising from the inability to maintain relationships stably in their desired condition (in 7th & 8th positions only; mild if not classed as an 'anxiety').

Psychological interpretation: sensitive, and susceptible to gentleness and delicacy of feeling, with a desire to blend into some sort of mystic fusion of erotic harmony. However, this desire remains unsatisfied due to the lack of a suitable partner or adverse conditions, and he keeps a strict and watchful control on his emotional relationships as he needs to know precisely where he stands. Is fastidious, aesthetic and has a cultured taste which allows him to form and express his own taste and judgement, especially in the fields of art and artistic creativity. Strives to ally with others who can assist him in his intellectual or artistic growth.

In brief: sublimated artistic sensitivity.

— 6 — 7
Brown/Black
6.3%

Physiological interpretation: stress resulting from unwelcome restriction or limitation (only significant if classed as an 'anxiety' in 7th & 8th positions; otherwise implies only the normal desire for independence).

Psychological interpretation: wants freedom to follow his own convictions and principals, to achieve respect as an individual in his own right. Desires to avail himself of every possible opportunity without having to submit to limitations or restrictions.

In brief: desire to control one's own destiny.

— 7 . . . . Black/. . . .

— 7
Black
35.1%

Physiological interpretation: stress arising from intensity (of feeling, endeavour, etc, as shown by the other colours). (Only of special significance if classed as an 'anxiety' in 8th position; otherwise normal.)

Psychological interpretation: wishes to be independent, unhampered and free from any limitation or restriction, other than those which he imposes on himself by his own choice and decision.

In brief: desire to control one's own destiny.

— 7 — 0
Black/Grey
10.5%

Physiological interpretation: pronounced susceptibility to outside stimuli (in 7th & 8th positions, but mainly if classed as an 'anxiety').

Psychological interpretation: wants to overcome a feeling of emptiness and of separation from others. Believes that life still has

far more to offer and that he may miss his share of experiences if he fails to make the best use of every opportunity. He therefore pursues his objectives with a fierce intensity and commits himself deeply and readily. Feels himself to be completely competent in any field in which he engages and can sometimes be considered by others to be interfering or meddlesome.
In brief: intense involvement.

— 7 — 1
Black/Blue
1.7%

Physiological interpretation: emotional dissatisfaction has given rise to a touchy and impatient desire for independence, leading to stress and restlessness (especially in 7th & 8th positions, but also in 6th & 7th).

Psychological interpretation: an existing situation or relationship is unsatisfactory, but he feels unable to improve it without willing cooperation. Unwilling to expose his vulnerability and therefore considers it inadvisable to display affection or be over-demonstrative. He regards the relationship as a depressing tie, but although he wants to be independent and unhampered, he does not want to risk losing anything. All this leads him to react touchily and with impatience, while the urge to get away results in considerable restlessness. The ability to concentrate may suffer.

In brief: restless instability arising from emotional dissatisfaction.

(The **+** group is therefore needed as a compensation.)

— 7 — 2
Black/Green
0.8%

Physiological interpretation: frustration at unacceptable restrictions on his freedom of action is producing stress (especially in 7th & 8th positions, but also in 6th & 7th).

Psychological interpretation: seeks independence and freedom from any restriction and therefore avoids obligations or anything which might prove hampering. He is being subjected to considerable pressure and wants to escape from it so that he can obtain what he needs, but tends to lack the necessary strength of purpose to succeed in this.
In brief: frustrated desire for independence and freedom of action.
(The **+** group is therefore needed as a compensation.)

    *

−7−3

Black/Red
.7%

Physiological interpretation: stress arising from the frustrations of an unwanted situation (especially in 7th & 8th positions, but also in 6th & 7th).
Psychological interpretation: feels trapped in a disagreeable situation and powerless to remedy it. Angry and disgruntled as he doubts that he will be able to achieve his goals, and frustrated almost to the point of nervous prostration. Wants to get away, to feel less restricted and be free to make his own decisions.
In brief: frustrated desire for independence.

    **

(The **+** group is therefore needed as a compensation.)

−7−4

Black/Yellow
.5%

Physiological interpretation: stress resulting from disappointment and watchful self-protection against further setback (especially in 7th & 8th positions, but also in 6th & 7th).

Psychological interpretation: **unfulfilled hopes have led to uncertainty and a tense watchfulness. Insists on freedom of action and resents any form of control other than that which is self-imposed. Unwilling to go without or to relinquish anything, and demands security as a protection against any further setback or loss of position and prestige. Doubts that things will be any better in the future, and this negative attitude leads him to exaggerate his claims and to refuse reasonable compromises.**

In brief: **watchful and retentive.**

(The + group is therefore needed as a compensation.)   *

— 7 — 5

Black/Violet
3.0%

Physiological interpretation: stress resulting from unwelcome restriction or limitation (in 7th & 8th positions, but mainly if classed as an 'anxiety').

Psychological interpretation: sensitive and impressionable, prone to absorbing enthusiasms. Seeks an idealized – but so far unfulfilled – situation in which he can share with another a complete accord and mutual depth of understanding. Feels there is a risk of being exploited if he is too ready to trust others and therefore demands proof of their sincerity. Needs to know exactly where he stands in his relationships.

In brief: demand for shared independence.

— 7 — 6

Black/Brown
3.5%

Physiological interpretation: stress resulting from unwelcome restriction or limitation (in 7th & 8th positions, but mainly if classed as an 'anxiety').

Psychological interpretation: resists any

form of pressure from others and insists on his independence as an individual. Wants to make up his own mind without interference, to draw his own conclusions and arrive at his own decisions. Detests uniformity and mediocrity. As he wants to be regarded as one who gives authoritative opinions, he finds if difficult to admit to being wrong, while at times he is reluctant to accept or understand another's point of view.

In brief: demand for independence and perfectionism.

TABLE V: + — FUNCTIONS
+ 0 — . . . . Grey/ . . .

+ 0 — 0

Grey/Grey

Denotes an ambivalent attitude varying between cautious reserve and the fear of not receiving his due.
(For additional details, see pp 47–8, 57–9).

+ 0 — 1

Grey/Blue

Anxiety and restless dissatisfaction, either with circumstances or with unfulfilled emotional requirements, have produced tension and stress. His attempt to escape from these consists of creating at least an outward semblance of peace by refusing to allow himself to be involved.
(For additional details, see pp 59–63, 57–9.)

*

+ 0 — 2

Grey/Green

Failure to establish himself in a manner consonant with his own high opinion of his worth, combined with the continued effort to prove himself with inadequate resources, have resulted in considerable stress. Tries to escape from these excessive demands on his meagre reserves by adopting a defensive attitude in which he refuses to be committed, or to be involved in further unpleasantness.
(For additional details, see pp 63–5, 57–9.)

+ 0 — 3

Grey/Red

Depleted vitality has created an intolerance for any further stimulation, or demands on his resources. A feeling of powerlessness subjects him to agitation,

Irritation and acute distress from which he
tries to escape by refusing further direct
participation. He confines himself to a cautious approach and a concealed determination to get his own way in the end.   ★★
(For additional details, see pp 65–8,
57–9.)

+ 0 — 4
Grey/Yellow

Disappointment at the non-fulfilment of
his hopes and the fear that to formulate
fresh goals will only lead to further setbacks have resulted in considerable
anxiety. He tries to escape from this by
withdrawing and protecting himself with
an attitude of cautious reserve. Moody and
depressed.   ★★
(For additional details, see pp 68–71,
57–9.)

+ 0 — 5
Grey/Violet

Needs to protect himself against his tendency to be too trusting, as he finds it is
liable to be misunderstood or exploited by
others. As a result, he adopts a critical
and stand-offish attitude, being willing
to participate only where he can be as-
sured of sincerity and trustworthiness.
(For additional details, see pp 57–9,
71–3.)

+ 0 — 6
Grey/Brown

The unsatisfied desire to be respected, to
stand out from amongst his fellows, is
causing some anxiety. As a result, normal
gregariousness is suppressed and he
refuses to allow himself to become involved, or to participate with others in
their ordinary activities.
(For additional details, see pp 57–9,
73–5.)

+ 0 − 7

Grey/Black

Fears that his independence will be threatened or severely restricted unless he protects himself from any outside influence. Does not want to be bothered.
(For additional details, see pp 57–9, 75–6.)

+1 − .. Blue/. ...

+1 − 1

Blue/Blue

Denotes an ambivalent attitude varying between a relaxed contentment and a restless dissatisfaction.
(For additional details, see pp 47–8, 59–63.)

+1 − 0

Blue/Grey

Needs to achieve a stable and peaceful condition, enabling him to free himself of the worry that he may be prevented from achieving all the things he wants.
(For additional details, see pp 57–9, 59–63.)

+1 − 2

Blue/Green

The tensions and stresses induced by trying to cope with conditions which are really beyond his capabilities or reserves of strength have led to considerable anxiety, and a sense of personal (but unadmitted) inadequacy. He seeks to escape into a more peaceful and problem-free situation, in which he will no longer have to assert himself or contend with so much pressure.   *
(For additional details, see pp 63–5, 59–63.)

+1 − 3

Blue/Red

Depleted vitality has created an intolerance for any further stimulation, or demands on his resources. A feeling of powerlessness subjects him to agitation and acute distress. Tries to escape from

this by relinquishing the struggle, and by finding peaceful and restful conditions in which to recuperate in an atmosphere of affection and security.   *
(For additional details, see pp 65–8, 59–63.)

+ 1 − 4
Blue/Yellow

Disappointment at the non-fulfilment of his hopes and the fear that to formulate fresh goals will only lead to further set-backs have resulted in considerable anxiety. He is trying to escape from this into a peaceful and harmonious relationship, protecting him from dissatisfaction and lack of appreciation.   *
(For additional details, see pp 68–71, 59–63.)

+ 1 − 5
Blue/Violet

Needs to protect himself against his tendency to be too trusting, as he finds it is liable to be misunderstood or exploited by others. Is therefore seeking a relationship providing peaceful and understanding intimacy, and in which each knows exactly where the other stands.
(For additional details, see pp 71–3, 59–63.)

+ 1 − 6
Blue/Brown

Wants to be valued and respected, and seeks this from a close and peaceful association of mutual esteem.
(For additional details, see pp 73–5, 59–63.)

+ 1 − 7
Blue/Black

Does not wish to be involved in differences of opinion, contention or argument, preferring to be left in peace.
(For additional details, see pp 75–6, 59–63.)

+ 2 − 2

Green/Green

Denotes an ambivalent attitude varying between self-insistence and the desire to escape the pressures which oppose it.
(For additional details, see pp 47–8, 63–5.)

+ 2 − 0

Green/Grey

Afraid that he may be prevented from achieving the things he wants and therefore demands that others should recognize his right to them.
(For additional details, see pp 57–9, 63–5.)

+ 2 − 1

Green/Blue

Anxiety and restless dissatisfaction, either with his circumstances or with unfulfilled emotional demands, have produced stress. He tries to escape from these by denying their existence, concealing his dissatisfaction behind a proud but illusory claim to self-sufficiency and independence.
(For additional details, see pp 59–63, 63–5.)

+ 2 − 3

Green/Red

Depleted vitality has created an intolerance for any further stimulation, or demands on his resources. This sense of powerlessness, combined with frustration that he cannot control events, subjects him to agitation, irritation and acute distress. He tries to escape from these by stubborn insistence on his own point of view, but the general condition of helplessness renders this often unsuccessful. Is therefore very sensitive to criticism and quick to take offence.
(For additional details, see pp 65–8, 63–5.)

+ 2 − 4

Green/Yellow

Disappointment and the fear that there is no point in formulating fresh goals have led to anxiety. Desires recognition and position, but is worried about his prospects. Reacts to this by protesting at any criticism and resisting any attempt to influence him. Tries to assert himself by meticulous control of detail in an effort to strengthen his position.

*

(For additional details, see pp 68–71, 63–5.)

+ 2 − 5

Green/Violet

Works to strengthen his position and bolster his self-esteem by examining his own accomplishments (and those of others) with critical appraisal and scientific discrimination. Insists on having things clear-cut and unequivocal.

(For additional details, see pp 71–3, 63–5.)

+ 2 − 6

Green/Brown

Needs to be valued and respected as an exceptional individual, in order to increase his self-esteem and his feeling of personal worth. Resists mediocrity and sets himself high standards.

(For additional details, see pp 73–5, 63–5.)

+ 2 − 7

Green/Black

Strongly resists outside influence and any interference with his freedom to make his own decisions and plans. Works to establish and strengthen his own position.

(For additional details, see pp 75–6, 63–5.)

+ 3 — 3

Red/Red

Denotes an ambivalent attitude varying between the desire to have his own way and the need to be left in peace.
(For additional details, see pp 47–8, 65–8.)

+ 3 — 0

Red/Grey

The fear that he may be prevented from achieving the things he wants leads him to play his part with an urgent and hectic intensity.
(For additional details, see pp 57–9, 65–8.)

+ 3 — 1

Red/Blue

Anxiety and a restless dissatisfaction, either with circumstances or with unful-filled emotional needs, have produced stress. He tries to escape by intense activity, directed either towards personal success or towards variety of experience.
(For additional details, see pp 59–63, 65–8.)

+ 3 — 2

Red/Green

The tensions induced by trying to cope with conditions which are really beyond his capabilities, or his reserves of strength, have led to considerable anxiety and to a sense of personal (but unadmitted) in-adequacy. He attempts to remedy this by intense activity and by insistence on get-ting his own way. Faulty self-control can lead to ungovernable displays of anger.
(For additional details, see pp 63–5, 65–8.)

+ 3 — 4

Red/Yellow

Disappointment and the fear that there is no point in formulating fresh goals have led to stress and anxiety. He wants con-genial contact with others and scope for

180

development, but feels that his relationships are empty and his progress impeded.
He reacts with an intense and zealous
activity designed to achieve his aims at all
costs.   *
(For additional details, see pp 68–71, 65–8.)

+ 3 — 5

Red/Violet

Wants to act freely and uninhibitedly, but
is restrained by his need to have things on
a rational, consistent and clearly-defined
basis.
(For additional details, see pp 71–3, 65–8.)

+ 3 — 6

Red/Brown

Takes a delight in action and wants to be
respected and esteemed for his personal
accomplishments.
(For additional details, see pp 73–5, 65–8.)

+ 3 — 7

Red/Black

Fights against restriction or limitation, and
insists on developing freely as a result
of his own efforts.
(For additional details, see pp 75–6,
65–8.)

+ 4 — . . Yellow/. . . .

+ 4 — 4

**Yellow/
Yellow**

Denotes an ambivalent attitude varying
between an optimistic desire for fulfilment
and a gloomy pessimism.
(For additional details, see pp 47–8, 68–71.)

+ 4 — 0

Yellow/Grey

The fear that he may be prevented from
achieving the things he wants leads him
into a restless search for satisfaction in
the pursuit of illusory or meaningless
activities.
(For additional details, see pp 57–9, 68–71.)

+ 4 — 1

Yellow/Blue

Anxiety and restless dissatisfaction, either with his circumstances or with unfulfilled emotional needs, have produced stress. He feels misunderstood, disoriented and unsettled. This drives him into a search for new conditions or relationships, in the hope that these might offer greater contentment and peace of mind.
(For additional details, see pp 59–63, 68–71.)

+ 4 — 2

Yellow/Green

The tensions induced by trying to cope with conditions which are really beyond his capabilities, or reserves of strength, have led to considerable anxiety and a sense of personal (but unadmitted) inadequacy. He reacts by seeking outside confirmation of his ability and value in order to bolster his self-esteem. Inclined to blame others so that he may shift the blame from himself. Anxiously searching for solutions and prone to compulsive inhibitions and compulsive desires.
(For additional details, see pp 63–5, 68–71.)

+ 4 — 3

Yellow/Red

Agitation, unpredictability and irritation accompanying depleted vitality and intolerance of further demands have all placed him in a position in which he feels menaced by his circumstances. Feeling powerless to remedy this by any action of his own, he is desperately hoping that some solution will provide a way of escape.
(For additional details, see pp 65–8, 68–71.)

+ 4 — 5

Yellow/Violet

Intensely critical of the existing conditions which he feels are disorganized or insufficiently clear-cut. Is therefore seeking some solution which will clarify the situa-

tion and introduce a more acceptable
degree of order and method.
(For additional details, see pp 71–3, 68–71.)

+ 4 — 6

Yellow/Brown

Feels insufficiently valued in his existing
situation, and is seeking different conditions in which he will have greater opportunity of demonstrating his worth.
(For additional details, see pp 73–5, 68–71.)

+ 4 — 7

Yellow/Black

Feels restricted and prevented from
progressing; seeking a solution which
will remove these limitations.
(For additional details, see pp 75–6, 68–71.)

+ 5 — . . Violet/. . . .

+ 5 — 5

Violet/Violet

Denotes an ambivalent attitude varying
between the desire for uncritical companionship and disdain of others for their
lack of taste and understanding.
(For additional details, see pp 47–8, 71–3.)

+ 5 — 0

Violet/Grey

Has a fear that he may be prevented from
achieving the things he wants. This leads
him to employ great personal charm in his
dealings with others, hoping that this will
make it easier for him to reach his objectives.
(For additional details, see pp 57–9, 71–3).

+ 5 — 1

Violet/Blue

Anxiety and a restless dissatisfaction,
either with his circumstances or with unfulfilled emotional needs, have produced
considerable stress. He tries to escape
into an idealized atmosphere of sympathy
and understanding, or into a substitute
environment of aestheticism and beauty.
(For additional details, see pp 59–63, 71–3.)

+ 5 — 2

Violet/Green

The tensions induced by trying to cope with conditions which are really beyond his capabilities, or reserves of strength, have led to considerable anxiety and a sense of personal (but unadmitted) inadequacy. He attempts to escape from this into a substitute world in which things are more nearly as he desires them to be.
(For additional details, see pp 63–5, 71–3.)

+ 5 — 3

Violet/Red

Depleted vitality has created an intolerance for any further stimulation, or demands on his resources. This feeling of powerlessness subjects him to agitation and acute distress. He attempts to escape from this into an illusory substitute world in which things are more nearly as he desires them to be.
(For additional details, see pp 65–8, 71–3.)

+ 5 — 4

Violet/Yellow

Disappointment and the fear that there is no point in formulating fresh goals have led to anxiety, and he is distressed by the lack of any close and understanding relationship. He attempts to escape into a substitute world in which these disappointments are submerged and things are more nearly as he desires them to be.
(For additional details, see pp 68–71, 71–3.)

+ 5 — 6

Violet/Brown

Greatly impressed by the unique, by originality and by individuals of outstanding characteristics. Tries to emulate the characteristics he admires and to display originality in his own personality.
(For additional details, see pp 73–5, 71–3.)

+ 5 − 7
Violet/Black

Seeks to avoid criticism and to prevent restriction of his freedom to act, and to decide for himself by the exercise of great personal charm in his dealings with others.
(For additional details, see pp 75–6, 71–3.)

+ 6 − . . Brown/. . . .

+ 6 − 6
Brown/Brown

Denotes an ambivalent attitude varying between a need for contented security and a desire for special recognition.
(For additional details, see pp 47–8, 73–5.)

+ 6 − 0
Brown/Grey

The fear that he may be prevented from achieving the things he wants increases his need for security and freedom from conflict. Is therefore seeking stability and an environment in which he can relax.
(For additional details, see pp 57–9, 73–5.)

+ 6 − 1
Brown/Blue

Anxiety and a restless dissatisfaction, either with circumstances or with unfulfilled emotional needs, have produced considerable stress. He tries to escape from these into a conflict-free security in which he can relax and recover. ★★
(For additional details, see pp 59–63, 73–5.)

+ 6 − 2
Brown/Green

The tensions induced by trying to cope with conditions which are really beyond his capabilities, or his reserves of strength, have led to considerable anxiety and a sense of personal (but unadmitted) inadequacy. He attempts to escape from this into a stable and secure environment in which he can relax and recover, free from any further demands on him. ★★
(For additional details, see pp 63–5, 73–5.)

+ 6 − 3

Brown/Red

Depleted vitality has created an intolerance for any further stimulation, or demands on his resources. This sense of powerlessness subjects him to agitation and acute distress. He attempts to escape into a stable and secure environment in which he can relax and recover. **
(For additional details, see pp 65–8, 73–5.)

+ 6 − 4

Brown/Yellow

Disappointment and the fear that there is no point in formulating fresh goals have led to anxiety, and he is distressed by the lack of any close and understanding relationship or adequate appreciation. He attempts to escape into a stable and secure environment in which he can relax and feel more contented. **
(For additional details, see pp 68–71, 73–5.)

+ 6 − 5

Brown/Violet

Wishes to safeguard himself against criticism or conflict and to entrench himself in a stable and secure position; but is himself inclined to be critical of others and difficult to please.
(For additional details, see pp 71–3, 73–5.)

+ 6 − 7

Brown/Black

Seeks security and a position in which he will no longer be troubled by demands being made on him.
(For additional details, see pp 75–6, 73–5.)

+ 7 − .. Black/....

+ 7 − 7

Black/Black

Denotes an ambivalent attitude varying between normal individualism and a stubborn denigration of any other viewpoint.
(For additional details, see pp 47–8, 75–6.)

+7−0

Black/Grey

The fear that he may be prevented from achieving the things he wants drives him to the exploitation of all types of experience, so that he may categorically deny that any of them has any value. This destructive denigration becomes his method of concealing hopelessness and a profound sense of futility.

(For additional details, see pp 57–9, 75–6.)

*

+7−1

Black/Blue

Anxiety and a restless dissatisfaction, either with circumstances or with unfulfilled emotional needs, have produced considerable stress. He reacts by putting this down to a total lack of understanding on the part of others, and by adopting a scornful and defiant attitude.

(For additional details, see pp 59–63, 75–6.)

**

+7−2

Black/Green

The tensions induced by trying to cope with conditions which are really beyond his capabilities, or his reserves of strength, have led to considerable anxiety and a sense of personal (but unadmitted) inadequacy. His inability to enforce his will causes him to over-react in stubborn defiance and by assigning to others all the blame for his own failures.

(For additional details, see pp 63–5, 75–6.)

**

+7−3

Black/Red

Depleted vitality has created an intolerance for any further stimulation, or demands on his resources. This feeling of powerlessness subjects him to agitation and acute distress. He reacts by considering that he has been victimized, and

insists – with indignation, resentment and
defiance – on being given his own way.   **
(For additional details, see pp 65–8,
75–6.)

+7 — 4

Black/Yellow

Disappointment and the fear that there is
no point in formulating fresh goals have
led to anxiety, emptiness and an unadmitted self-contempt. His refusal to admit
this leads to his adopting a headstrong
and defiant attitude.   **
(For additional details, see pp 68–71, 75–6.)

+7 — 5

Black/Violet

His natural ability to examine everything
with critical discrimination has been dis-
torted into an attitude of harsh disappro-
val, which opposes and denigrates without
regard to the real facts.   *
(For additional details, see pp 71–3, 75–6.)

+7 — 6

Black/Brown

The need for esteem – for the chance to
play some outstanding part and make a
name for himself – has become imperative. He reacts by insisting on being the
centre of attention, and refuses to play an
impersonal or minor role.   *
(For additional details, see pp 73–5, 75–6.)

Appendices

APPENDIX A

ALLOCATION OF Is IN A SAMPLE OF 1,000 'NORMAL' ADULTS *

No of Is	No of adults selecting	PERCENTAGE with 'better' choice	with 'worse' choice	
0	259	0	74.1	
1	122	25.9	61.9	Approx
—2 —	143 —	38.1 —	47.6 —	Average
3	117	52.4	35.9	
4	86	64.1	27.3	
5	91	72.7	18.2	
6	55	81.8	12.7	
7	48	87.3	7.9	
8	34	92.1	4.5	
9	24	95.5	2.1	
10	14	97.9	0.7	
11	6	99.3	0.1	
12	1	99.9	0	

Total: 1,000

No attempt has been made in this table to distinguish between age or sex. The sole criterion of 'normality' used is that all of the 1,000 persons of the sample were actually engaged in earning their livings in various types of employment, ranging from presidents of multi-billion dollar concerns to workers on the factory floor.

* 'Normal' British adults of both sexes, employed in commerce and industry in the United Kingdom (data: I. Scott).

APPENDIX B

OPTIMUM AND SUB-OPTIMUM FUNCTIONAL GROUPS AS SHOWN BY ALLOCATION OF *'s

Reproduced from Tables I, II, III, IV and V.

No * represents no conflict or minimal conflict
1 * represents some conflict, not necessarily serious (*)
2 *s represent appreciable conflict (**)
3 *s represent serious conflict (***)

(but in all cases, the overall interpretation must be borne in mind).

+ Function		× Function		= Function		− Function		+ − Function	
0 *	4 *	0 *	4	0	4	0 **	4 **		40 **
01 *	40 **	01	40	01	40	01 **	40 *	01 **	41 **
02 *	41 *	02	41	02	41	02 **	41***	02 **	42 **
03 *	42 *	03	42	03 *	42	03 **	42***	03 **	43 **
04 **	43 *	04	43	04	43 *	04 **	43***	04 **	45
05 *	45 *	05	45	05	45	05	45 *	05	46
06 **	46 **	06 **	46	06	46	06	46 *	06	47
07***	47***	07 *	47 *	07	47	07	47 *	07	

190

* * * *	** ** ** **	* ** ** ** * *
50	60	70
51	61	71
52	62	72
53	63	73
54	64	74
56	65	75
57	67	76

* * *	* * *	* * *
10	20	30
12	21	31
13	23	32
14	24	34
15	25	35
16	26	36
17	27	37

* * **	* * ** *	* * ** *
5	6	7
50	60	70
51	61	71
52	62	72
53	63	73
54	64	74
56	65	75
57	67	76

* *** *** * *	** ** *** *** * *	** ** *** *** ** * *
1	2	3
10	20	30
12	21	31
13	23	32
14	24	34
15	25	35
16	26	36
17	27	37

*	*	*
5	6	7
50	60	70
51	21	71
52	62	72
53	63	73
54	64	74
56	65	75
57	67	76

*	*	* * * * * * *
1	2	3
10	20	30
12	21	31
13	23	32
14	24	34
15	25	35
16	26	36
17	27	37

* * *	* * *	* ** * * * * **
5	6	7
50	60	70
51	61	71
52	62	72
53	63	73
54	64	74
56	65	75
57	67	76

*	*	*
1	2	3
10	20	30
12	21	31
13	23	32
14	24	34
15	25	35
16	26	36
17	27	37

* * * **	* ** * * * * * ***	** *** ** ** *** ** ***
5	6	7
50	60	70
51	61	71
52	62	72
53	63	73
54	64	74
56	65	75
57	67	76

* * **	* * **	* * **
1	2	3
10	20	30
12	21	31
13	23	32
14	24	34
15	25	35
16	26	36
17	27	37

LITERATURE ABOUT THE LÜSCHER COLOUR TEST

J. Aström and E. Tobiason — 'A Clinical Trial of the Lüscher Colour Test', *Medico* (Boehringer Mannheim) 1965, Nr. 2, 53.

J. G. H. Bokslag — 'After und Geschlecht im Lüscher-Test und der Einfluss des Versuchsleiters', *Ausdruckskunde* 2, 1955, 34.

J. G. H. Bokslag — 'Leeftijd en Geslacht bij de Lüscher-Test en de Invloed van de Proefleider', *Nederlandsch Tijdschrift voor de Psychologie en haar Grensgebieden* 6, 1954, 497.

J. G. H. Bokslag — 'Die anamnestisch verzeichnete Religion im Lüscher-Test', *Psychologia Religionis*, Basel 1956, Nr. 2.

L. Busch — 'Der chronische Alkoholismus im Lücher-Farbtest', *Medizinische Klinik* 59, 1964, 254.

L. Busch — 'Die physiologischen Komponenten bei farbpsychologischen Untersuchungen', *Die Medizinische Welt* 1965, 2582.

N. Canivet — 'Le test de Lüscher', *Bulletin de Psychologie*, Nr. 225, tome XVII 2–7, Paris 1963, 322–6.

W. Canziani — 'Zur Entwicklung der Ehekonflikte', *Der Psychologe* 10, 1958, 132.

W. Canziani — 'Zur Funktionspsychologie der Ehekonflikte', *Heilpäd. Werkblätter*, Lucerne 1962, Nr. 2.

H. Cardinaux	'Verhaltensweisen hospitalisierter Kinder', Dissertation (leading to the diploma) at the Institute for Abnormal Children of Freiburg University, Switzerland, 1967.
M. Clerici	'Contributo allo studio del test cromatico de Lüscher', *Riv. Ital. di Med. e igiene della scuola,* vol. VI, fasc. II, 1960.
E. A. Cohn	*Der 8-Farbentest in seiner heutigen Form.* Berlin 1968.
H. Dietschy and N. Dietschy	'Farbwahl und Charakter von zentralbrasilianischen Indianern', *Acta tropica,* Basel, 15, 1958, 241.
F. Dittmar	'Affektstörungen bei der vegetativen Dystonie', *Verhandl. Dtsch. Ges. Inn. Med.* 68, 1962, 129.
W. Eggert	'Eine neue Methode zur Objektivierung der vegetativen Störungen', *Medizinische Welt* 1965, Nr. 3, 155.
W. Eggert	'Wirkungsnachweis zentraler Regulatoren bei vegetativen Funktionstörungen mit Hilfe des Lüscher-Tests', *Medizinische Welt* 1967, 65.
W. Eggert	'Diagnostik funktioneller Syndrome mit dem Lüscher-Farbtest', Scientific Supplement to *Materia Medica,* Nordmark 1965, Nr. 54.
J. Erbslöh	'Über die Erkennungsmöglichkeit der Dyspareunie im Farbentest', *Die Medizinische Welt* 1955, Nr. 51, 1769.
J. Erbslöh	'Die Adipositas und ihre Behandlung aus der Sicht der Farbenpsychologie', *Die Medizinische Welt* 1957, Nr. 10, 349.

J. Erbslöh   'Der Lüscher-Farbtest', *Die Medizinische Welt* 1956, 363.

J. Erbslöh   'L'application du Test de Lüscher dans le cadre de la préparation psychologique à l'accouchement', 'The applicability of the Lüscher-Test in psychological preparation for delivery', 'Über die Anwendung des Lüscher-Tests im Rahmen der psychologischen Geburtsvorbereitung', *Médicine psychosomatique et maternité. Revue de médicine psychosomatique*, Paris 1962.

J. Erbslöh and I. Lüscher   'Die Bedeutung des Lüscher-Tests für die Beurteilung seelischer Veränderungen während der Gestationsperiode', *Medizinische Welt* 1962, Nr. 40, 2087.

J. Erbslöh   'Die Verwendung des Lüscher-Farbtests in der ärztlichen Praxis', *Ärztliche Praxis* 1962, Nr. 31, 1619.

J. Erbslöh   'Farbenpsychologie, Farbentherapie und Farberziehung', Scientific Supplement to *Materia Medica,* Nordmark 1964, Nr. 51.

J. Erbslöh   'Die Verwendung des Lüscher-Farbtests in der ärztlichen Praxis', *Der niedergelassene Arzt* 11, 1962, Nr. 12, 30.

K. Flehinghaus   'Innere Gestimmtheit und Farb-Umwelt des Kindes. Ergebnisse einer Untersuchung an 1000 Volksschulkindern', *Praxis der Kinderpsychologie und Kinderpsychiatrie* 8, 1959, 231.

K. Flehinghaus   'Die Signifikanzprüfung des Lüscher-Tests bei Volksschulkindern', *Praxis der Kinderpsychologie und Kinderpsychiatrie* 10, 1961, 143.

E. Franzen   *Testpsychologie.* Ullstein-Paperback Nr. 181, Berlin 1958.

W. Furrer   *Die Farbe in der Persönlichkeits-Diagnostik.* Lüscher-Test Textbook. Test-Verlag, Basel 1953.

W. Furrer   'Der Lüscher-Test'; in: E. Stern, *Die Tests in der klinischen Psychologie,* Vol I, Part 2, Rascher-Verlag, Zürich 1955.

W. Furrer   'Die Farbe als Testmittel', *Schweiz. Archiv Neurologie, Neurochirurgie und Psychiatrie* 95, 1965, 189.

W. Furrer   'Psychiatrische Testverfahren, besonders Lüscher-Farbtest', *Therapie der Gegenwart* 106, 1967, 1290.

G. Gerster   *Eine Stunde mit...Besuche in der Werkstatt des Wissens.* Ullstein-Paperback Nr. 73, Berlin 1956, appeared also in: *Die Weltwoche,* Zürich, 23. 1. 1955.

G. Gerster   'Psychologie der Kleuren', *De Kern* (Nederlandse Digest) 1957, Nr. 12.

L. Goldschmidt   'Lieblingsfarben bei Kindern?' *Zeitschr. für Heilpädagogik,* Januar 1953.

L. Goldschmidt   'Farben als psychologisches Untersuchungsmittel?' *Zeitschrift für Heilpädagogik* 1951, 412.

L. Goldschmidt   'Beispiele aus der Praxis mit dem Lüscher-Test', *Zeitschrift für Heilpädagogik,* Februar 1952, 65.

H. Gramm   'Farbpsychologische Alternsstudien im Lichte der Statistik', *Zeitschrift für Alternsforschung* 14, 1960, 2.

P. Grof E. Svitavska and M. Vojtechovský	Vliv Phenoharmanu na emocni zmeny vyvolané aplikaci vyšších davek Dexfenmetrazinu. Sbornik IX. celostatni psychiatrické konference v Karlovych Varech 1961.
W. Groh	'Die Bedeutung von Physiotherapie und Funktionspsychologie für Gesundheitsvorsorge und Prävention', *Physikal. Med. u. Rehabil.* 12, 1968, 327.
W. Groh	'Anleitung zum Lüscher-Test', *Ärztliche Praxis* 16, 1969, 903.
P. Haelg	'Die Bedeutung der über- und unterwertigen Kolonnen im Lüscher-Test für die pädagogische Führung', Dissertation (leading to the diploma) at the Institute for Abnormal Children of Freiburg University, Switzerland, 1967.
P. Haelg	'Erfolgs- und Misserfolgserlebnis nach einer Schulleistungsprüfung', Dissertation (leading to the diploma) at the Institute for Abnormal Children of Freiburg University, Switzerland, 1968.
E. M. Hilgers	'Lüscher's Kleurentest. Een Introductie'; 'Lüschers Farbtest. Eine Einführung'. Gawein. *Tijdschrift van de Psychologische Kring aan de Nijmeegse Universiteit* 3, 1955, 153.
A. Kessler	'Expériences d'administration collective des tests de Koch (test de l'arbre) et de Lüscher (test de couleur)', *Orientamenti Pedagogici* 1968, Nr. 86, 333.
H. Klar	'Farbpsychologische Untersuchung von 1000 Persern. (Vergleich mit Europäern in Persien.)' *Acta Tropica,* Basel 15, 1958, Nr. 3, 234.

H. Klar	'L'ivresse de l'opium à la lumière du test des couleurs. Examen psychologique de 70 fumeurs d'opium, pratiqué avant et après l'usage du stupéfiant, au moyen de l'é preuve des couleurs', *Médecine et Hygiène,* Genève 17, 1959, Nr. 427, 20. 4. 1959.
H. Klar	*Die Dokumentation des Lüscher-Farbtests mit Handlochkarten.* Ordo-Verlag, Stuttgart 1960.
H. Klar	Ihre Lieblingsfarbe gibt Auskunft. Der Lüscher-Farbtest und sein medizinischer Anwendungsbereich. Selecta 2, 1960, Nr. 18, 16.
H. Klar	'Der Lüscher-Farbtest – ein besonders zuverlässiges Verfahren in der Psychodiagnostik funktioneller Erkrankungen', *Therapie des Monats* (Boehringer Mannheim) 1960, Nr. 5, 214.
H. Klar	'The Lüscher-Colour-Test – a Highly Reliable Procedure in the Psychodiagnostics of Functional Disorders', *Medico* (Boehringer Mannheim) 1961, Nr. 4.
H. Klar	'Le test des couleurs de Lüscher – une méthode particulièrement efficace dans le psychodiagnostic des maladies fonctionnelles', *Medico* (Boehringer Mannheim) 1961, Nr. 4.
H. Klar	'El test cromatico de Lüscher – un método particularmente exacto para el psicodiagnostico de los trastornos funcionales', *Medico* (Boehringer Mannheim) 1961, Nr. 4.
H. Klar and J. S. Endres	'Farben helfen heilen', (4 colour reproductions), *Therapie des Monats* (Boehringer Mannheim) 1960, Nr. 5, 228.

| H. Klar | 'Colour Psychology and Medicine (1) Colours Do Not Lie', *Medico* (Boehringer Mannheim) 1961, Nr. 1. (Article also published in French and Spanish, *Medico* 1961, Nr. 1.) |

| H. Klar | 'Die Adipositas im Lichte des Farbtests', *Medico – European Edition* (Boehringer Mannheim) 1963, Nr. 2. |

| H. Klar | 'Obesity in the Light of the of the Colour Test', *Medico* (Boehringer Mannheim), 1961, Nr. 3. (Article also published in French and Spanish, *Medico* 1961, Nr. 3.) |

| H. Klar | 'Über Opiumraucher und ihre psychischen Veränderungen unmittelbar nach dem Rauchen', *Medico – European Edition* (Boehringer Mannheim) 1964, Nr. 5, 136. |

| H. Klar | 'Opium Smokers and the Psychological and Emotional Changes that take place immediately after Smoking', *Medico* (Boehringer Mannheim) 1962, Nr. 1. (Article also published in French, Spanish, and Italian, *Medico* 1962, Nr. 1.) |

| H. Klar | 'An Aid in Diagnosing Frigidity: the Lüscher Colour Test', *Medico* (Boehringer Mannheim) 1962, Nr. 2. (Article also published in French, Spanish, and Italian, *Medico* 1962, Nr. 2.) |

| H. Klar | 'Farbpsychologie und Medizin. Vom Fingerabdruck der Seele', *Medico – European Edition* (Boehringer Mannheim) 1963, Nr. 1. |

| H. Klar and R. Gortz | Über die psychischen Unterschiede bei schwangeren und nichtschwangeren Frauen', *Ärztliche Praxis* 16, 1964 and *Medico – European Edition* (Boehringer Mannheim) 1963, Nr. 4. |

H. Klar and R. Gortz	'The Emotional and Psychological Differences between Pregnant and Non-pregnant Women', *Medico* (Boehringer Mannheim) 1963, Nr. 2. (Article also published in French, Spanish, and Italian, *Medico* 1963, Nr. 2.)
H. Klar	'Der Lüscher-Farbtest, eine besonders zuverlässige und zeitsparende Methode zur Persönlichkeitsbeurteilung. (Tab. + +)', *Medico – European Edition* (Boehringer Mannheim) 1963, Nr. 5.
H. Klar	'Colour Psychology and Medicine (Tab + +)', *Medico* (Boehringer Mannheim) 1963, Nr. 3 (Article also published in French, Spanish, and Italian, *Medico* 1963, Nr. 3.)
H. Klar	'Zur Aufdeckung der krankmachenden Konfliktursachen mit dem Lüscher-Test. (Tab + −)', *Medico - European Edition* (Boehringer Mannheim) 1964, Nr. 2.
H. Klar	'The Discovery of Pathogenic Sources of Conflict by means of the Lüscher Test. (Tab + −)', *Medico* (Boehringer Mannheim) 1964, Nr. 2. (Article also published in French and Spanish, *Medico* 1964, Nr. 2.)
H. Klar	'Zur Prophylaxe der psychisch bedingten Fettsucht. Die Chi-Quadrat-Methode beim Lüscher-Farbtest', *Medizinische Welt* 1965, Nr. 3, 150.
H. Klar	'The Prophylactic Treatment of Psychogenic Adiposity. The Chi-Square Method in the Lüscher Colour Test', *Medico* (Boehringer Mannheim) 1966, Nr. 1. (Article also published in Spanish, *Medico* 1966, Nr. 1.)

| H. Klar | 'Colour Psychological Test on Examination Anxiety', *Medico* (Boehringer Mannheim) 1965, Nr. 4. (Article also published in Spanish, *Medico* 1965, Nr. 4.) |

| H. Klar | 'Die sexuelle Verführbarkeit debiler Kinder', *Ärztliche Praxis* 20, 1968, Nr. 39, 1862 |

| H. Klar | 'Liability to Sexual Seduction. Examination of Backward Children with the Lüscher Test', *Medico* (Boehringer Mannheim) 1968, Nr. 9. (Article also published in Spanish, *Medico* 1968, Nr. 9.) |

| H. Klar | 'Verlaufsstudie über 15 Jahre mit dem Lüscher-Test', *Selecta* 10, 1968, Nr. 39, 2486. |

| H. Klar | 'Reintegration Difficulties for Europeans after their Return from Development Countries', *Medico* (Boehringer Mannheim) 1968, Nr. 10. (Article also published in Spanish, *Medico* 1968, Nr. 10.) |

| H. Klar | 'Angst und Hoffnung der Vietnam-Rückwanderer', *euro-med* 8, 1968, Nr. 20, 1070. |

| H. Klar | 'Hope and Fear in Returnees from Vietnam', *Medico* (Boehringer Mannheim) 1968, Nr. 11. (Article also published in Spanish, *Medico* 1968, Nr. 11.) |

| S. Leedy P. Leroux J. Toncray M. Weiss | Maudsley Personality Inventory and Lüscher Colour Test. Psychology Laboratory and Research. Transylvania College Lexington, Kentucky, Spring 1962. |

| M. Lüscher | 'La couleur, moyen auxiliare de psychodiagnostic' in *Le diagnostic du caractère* Presses Universitaires de France, 1949. |

M. Lüscher	*Psychologie der Farben.* Test-Verlag, Basel 1949.
M. Lüscher	'Die ganzheitliche Deutung', *Ausdruckskunde,* Heidelberg, Volume 1, 1954, Heft 4/5.
M. Lüscher	*Psychologie und Psychotherapie als Kultur.* Test-Verlag, Basel 1955.
M. Lüscher	*Lüscher-Test. Anleitung und Farbtafeln. Klinischer Test zur psychosomatischen Persönlichkeitsdiagnostik.* Test-Verlag, Basel 1948.
M. Lüscher	'Farbenpsychologie', *Palette.* Sandoz AG, Basel, Spring 1959, Nr. 1.
M. Lüscher	'Einführung in die neuen Methoden der tiefenpsychologischen Werbegestaltung', *Kriterion* 1959, Nr. 3 und Nr. 4.
M. Lüscher	'Verständnis und Mibverständnis in der Psychologie der Farben', *Mensch und Farbe* 1959, Nr. 1, and also published by Test-Verlag, Basel.
M. Lüscher	'Verpackungsgestaltung und Farbpsychologie', *Palette.* Sandoz AG, Basel 1960, Nr. 5, 1.
M. Lüscher	'Die Methode der strukturellen Funktionspsychologie', *Heilpädagogische Werkblätter* 1962, Nr. 2, Lucerne, Separata by Test-Verlag, Basel.
M. Lüscher	'Die Farbwahl als psychosomatischer Test', *Dtsch. Med. Journal* 12, 1961, Nr. 11, 406.
M. Lüscher	'Die Farbgestaltung in der Industrie', *Die Wirtschaft* 1958, Nr. 2, Universum Press, Geneva/Zürich.

| M. Lüscher | 'Psychodiagnostik affektiver und vegeta-tiver Störungen', *Ärztliche Praxis* 15, 1963, Nr. 42, 2293. |

M. Lüscher   'Beiträge zum Farbtest nach Lüscher. Anleitung zum Lüscher-Farbtest', Scientific Supplement to *Materia Medica,* Nordmark, November 1965, Nr. 54.

M. Lüscher   Colour – the mother tongue of the unconscious. Parke-Davis. Monographie Nr. 5, Capsugel S.A., Basel.

I. Löffler and
E. Weiser   'Messung der Examensangst bei 200 Abiturienten', *Ärztliche Praxis* 17, 1965, Nr. 11, 537.

M. Maier   'Farbe und Charakter', *Im Dienste der Gesundheit,* Basel 1956, Nr. 1, 7–12. (Article also published in French, *La vie saine,* June 1956.)

M. Maier   'Farbe und Charakter Im Lüscher-Test', *Ausdruckskunde* 1, 1954, 209.

A. Mogensen and
N. Juel-Nielsen   'Factors Influencing Preference Rankings in a Special Picture Test and in Lüscher's Colour Test: A Study of Uniovular Twins Brought Up Apart', *Acta Psychiatria Scandinavica* 38, 1962, Nr. 3, 208.

N. Juel-Nielsen   'Wie reagiert der Homoerot auf Farben?' *Der Kreis,* Monatsschrift, Zürich, 1951, Nr. 19, 27.

M. Parejo   'Untersuchungen über die Psychologie der Farbe', *Acta med.* Tenerife, 1956, Nr. 6, 171.

| H. Paul | Personality study of former prisoners of war and former internees. Appearing in: 'Later Effects of Imprisonment and Deportation', International Conference organized by the World Veterans Federation, The Hague, Nov. 20th–25th, 1961, 101. |

| H. Paul | 'Der Lüscher-Farbtest', *Zentralblatt für Arbeitswissenschaft*, 1962, Nr. 10/12. |

| H. T. Piebenga | *Frequentie verdelingen van de kleurkeuzen bij 400 Friezen door.* Test-Verlag, Basel 1955. |

| H. T. Piebenga | *Frequenzverteilung der Farbwahlen bei 400 Friesen.* Test-Verlag, Basel 1955. |

| F. Preiswerk | *Intelligenz-Leistungstabellen zum Lüscher-Test.* Wilfriedstr. 2, Zürich, Selbstverlag, 1960. |

| F. Preiswerk | 'Analyse und Förderung der Intelligenzleistung auf Grund des Lüscher-Tests', *Der Psychologe* 1956, 471. |

| J. H. Prill and Ch. Oppelt | 'Die prognostische Beurteilung des Geburtsverhaltens durch den Lüscher-Test', Dissertation, University Clinic for Women, Würzburg 1962. |

| W. Ries | 'Das Altern in farbpsychologischer Sicht. Psychoexperimentelle Untersuchungen mit dem Lüscher-Test', *Zeitschr. für Alternsforschung* 13, 1959, 237. |

| W. Ries and J. Ulrich | 'Die Psyche der Fettsüchtigen im Lüscher-Farbtest', *Die Medizinische Welt*, 1959, Nr. 16, 777. |

| W. Ries and H. Gramm | 'Farbpsychologische Alternsstudien im Lichte der Statistik', *Zeitschr. für Alternsforschung* 14, 1960, Nr. 2, 113. |

P. Rokusfalvy   Palyavalaszto fiatalok érzelmi életének visszatükröződése a pszichologiai vizsgalatok adataiban.
Emotional Life of Young People Choosing a Profession as Reflected in the Data of Psychological Examinations.
Pszichologiai Tanulmanyok. cimü 1963. évi V. Kötetéböl, Budapest 1963.

P. Rokusfalvy   Az affektivitas szerepe a gépkocsivezetöjelöltek szenzomotoros teljesitményeinek alakulasaban.
The Part of Affectivity in the Formation of Sensomotoric Accomplishments of Motorcar-Driver Candidates.
Pszichologiai Tanulmanyok. cimü 1963. évi V. Kötetéböl, Budapest 1963.

P. Scherer   'Die Affektivität von Kranken mit organischer Hirnschädigung im Lüscher-Test', Dissertation (leading to the diploma) at the Institute for Abnormal Children of Freiburg University, Switzerland, 1969.

H. G. Schmidt   'Wege der Daignostik und Therapie bei psychogenen Krankheitszuständen', *Medizin heute* 5, 1956, 70.

H. G. Schmidt   'Psychische Faktoren bei Cholezystopathien', *Ärztliche Praxis* 1956, Nr. 24.

H. G. Schmidt   'Psychosomatik, Farbe und Homöopathie', *Erfahrungsheilkunde* 7, 1958, Nr. 2, 49.

H. G. Schmidt   'Wirkung der Farbe – Erkenntnis durch Farbe – aus ärztlicher Sicht', *Mensch nud Farbe* 1959, 45.

H. G. Schmidt   'Der Lüscher-Farbtest zur Diagnose der vegetativen Störungen', *Die Therapiewoche* 17, 1967, 642.

J. A. Schneider   'Farbwahl und Krankheit', *Die medizinische Welt* 1962, Nr. 43, 2279.

J. A. Schneider   'Der Lüscher-Farbtest in der ärztlichen Praxis', *Med. Klin.* 59, 1964, Nr. 28, 1127.

J. A. Schneider   'Farbwahl, Krankheit und vegetative Steuerung', *Med. Klin.* 59, 1964, Nr. 37, 1460.

H. Schoch-Bodmer   'Zur Problemanalyse von Kinderzeichnungen mit Lüschertest-Farben', *Der Psychologe (Ges. f. ges. u. prakt. Lebensgestaltung)* 4, 1952, 503.

I. A. Scott   The Lüscher Colour Personality Test – A Statistical Evaluation. 24 Somali Road, London NW2, England.

I. A. Scott   Making the most of manpower – Know more about man!

W. C. M. Smits and J. Stakenburg   'Instructie voor de Lüscher-Test', *Uitgave Bureau Experimenteel Testmateriaal.* Oranjesingel 3, Nimwegen 1958.

N. Spirig   'Der Lüscher-Test bei Maturanden mit gleichem Berufsziel', Dissertation (leading to the diploma) at the Institute for Abnormal Children of Freiburg University, Switzerland.

J. Spranger and J. Dörken   'Kindliche Adipositas: Prüfung der Psychodynamik unter d-Norpseudo-ephedrin', *Monatsschrift für Kinderheilkunde* 114, 1966, Nr. 7, 394.

L. Steinke   'Farbpsychologische Untersuchungen mit dem Lüscher-Test bei angeborenen Farbsinnstörungen', Dissertation, University Eye Clinic, Basel, 1960.

E. Stern and W. Furrer   *Die Tests in der klinischen Psychologie.* II Vol Rascger-Verlag, Zürich 1955.

H. Stockli   'Die Beziehungsschwache im Lüscher-Test', Dissertation (leading to the diploma) at the Institute for Abnormal Children of Freiburg University, Switzerland, 1967.

H. Storath   'Die Bedeutung der Farbe und ihre Anwendung im Lüscher-Test', *Der Psychologe* 4, 1952, Nr. 9, 358.

J. Ulrich   'Farbpsychologische Untersuchungen an fettsüchtigen Frauen mit Hilfe des Lüscher-Tests', Dissertation at the Karl Marx University, Leipzig, 1958.

H. Wallnöfer   'Der Lüscher-Test als zeitsparendes Hilfsmittel in der Allgemeinpraxis', *Österreichische Ärztezeitung* 19, 1964, Nr. 16.

H. Wallnöfer   'Der Lüscher-Farbtest zur Diagnose des vegetativen Verhaltens', *Ärztliche Praxis*, 18, 1966, Nr. 70, 2348.

H. Wallnöfer   *Die autogene Norm des Lüscher-Tests zur Kontrolle des Therapieerfolgs*, 1969.

H. Wallnöfer   *Seele ohne Angst.* Hoffmann und Campe-Verlag, Hamburg, 1968.

H. Wallnöfer   'Der Lüscher-Test im Vergleich zweier Privatpraxen', *Österreichische Ärztezeitung* 24, 1969, Nr. 5, 530.

H. Wohlfarth   'Versuche zur Bestimmung eines eventuellen Effektes von Farbstimuli auf das autonome Nervensystem', *Psychotherapie*, 1, 1956, 216.

H. Wohlfarth   'Psychophysische Auswertung der Versuche zur Bestimmung eines evtl. Effektes von Farbstimuli auf das autonome Nervensystem,' *Psychotherapie* 2, 1957, 86.

A. Zehnder 'Schwererziehbarkeit im Lüscher-Test. Eine Untersuchung an schwererziehbaren männlichen Jugendlichen', Dissertation (leading to the diploma) at the Institute for Abnormal Children of Freiburg University, Switzerland, 1953.

G. Zerbe 'Das Chromopsychogramm des Lüscher-Tests nach Dr. Zerbe/Dr. Klar und seine klinische Anwendung'. Address delivered to the IV International Congress for Cybernetic Medicine in Nice, September 19th–22nd, 1966.

G. Zerbe 'Farbe und Strukfur; strukturpsychologische Diagnostik I', *Der Landarzt,* Nr. 12, 1968.

H. Zgraggen 'Der Lüscher-Test bei milieugestorten Kindern', Dissertation (leading to the diploma) at the Institute for Abnormal Children of Freiburg University, Switzerland, 1967.

M. Zinder 'Die gebräuchlichsten Testmethoden in der Psychiatrie. Der Lüscher-Test', *Die moderne Psychiatrie,* Göttingen 1957, Nr. 5.

Übersetzungen des Lüscher-Tests und Referate sind in folgenden Sprachen Veröffentlicht worden: Deutsch, Englisch, Französisch, Spanisch, Italienisch, Holländisch, Ungarisch, Tschechisch, Portugiesisch.

Thomas A. Harris
I'm OK, You're OK 80p

This practical guide to Transactional Analysis is a unique approach to
your problems. Hundreds of thousands of people have found this
phenomenal breakthrough in psychotherapy a turning point in their
lives.
In sensible, non-technical language Thomas Harris explains how to
gain control of yourself, your relationships and your future – *no matter
what has happened in the past.*

Julius Fast
Body Language 70p

Every move you make reveals a secret . . . This important book adds a
new dimension to human understanding. Julius Fast teaches how to
penetrate the personal secrets of strangers, friends and lovers by
interpreting their body movements – and how to make use of the power
thus gained.

Mildred Nemman & Bernard Berkowitz
How to be Your Own Best Friend 35p

This remarkable book, written with warmth, understanding and
wisdom, provides simple guidelines to help you become the person it is in
you to be.
'There is no pill made that is as simple, effective and fast-working . . .
positively inspirational' NEIL SIMON